ADVENTURE TO
EVEREST BASE CAMP

Karl H. Myers

Title of Work: Adventure to Everest Base Camp

Copyright © 2017 by Karl H. Myers

The author can be reached at karlcsr@yahoo.com.

Cover photo by Karl H. Myers
Printed in the United States
http://www.createspace.com

ISBN-13: 978-1541379169
ISBN-10: 1541379160

Dedicated to Chhiring Passang Sherpa and Ang Kaji Sherpa.
This adventure would not have been possible without them.

Chhiring Passang Sherpa can be contacted at
chhiring110@gmail.com.

Ang Kaji Sherpa can be contacted on Facebook.

INDEX

CONCEPTION 7

BACKGROUND 12

THE PLAN 25

PREPARATION 29

DAY 1 – FLIGHT TOWARD LUKLA.................... 39

DAY 2 – HIKE TO NAMCHE BAZAAR 61

DAY 3 – NAMCHE BAZAAR................................ 79

DAY 4 – NAMCHE BAZAAR TO TENGBOCHE/DEBOCHE .. 99

DAY 5 – DEBOCHE TO DINGBOCHE 113

DAY 6 – DINGBOCHE 127

DAY 7 – DINGBOCHE TO LOBUCHE 136

DAY 8 – LOBUCHE TO GORAK SHEP AND BEYOND........ 150

DAY 9 – GORAK SHEP TO PANGBOCHE.............. 165

DAY 10 – PANGBOCHE TO NAMCHE BAZAAR 176

DAY 11 – NAMCHE BAZAAR TO LUKLA............... 181

DAY 12 – STRANDED IN LUKLA 192

DAY 13 – STRANDED IN LUKLA 206

DAY 14 – ESCAPE FROM LUKLA....................... 211

EPILOGUES 221

Conception

So what is the difference between a fantasy and a plan? When is that precise moment when that fantasy starts to become reality?

I almost feel like I tricked myself into making the transition. I was all fantasy, no action.

I have always enjoyed camping and hiking in the mountains. I have never lost that interest, although the past decade has been filled with more trips to the beach than to the mountains.

So it wasn't out of character to start watching YouTube videos of rock climbing and mountain climbing when I figured out how to project YouTube videos from my iPad 2 onto my new 65-inch television screen.

Of course, eventually, I worked my way to the mountain of all mountains, Mount Everest. A number of the videos were on climbing to the top of this big rock.

But then I started to watch videos of the classic hike from Lukla to Everest Base Camp, an adventure in itself -- and within the reach of mere mortals. All one needed was a few weeks of time and a bit of determination and physical fitness. If not one, at least the other.

And then a slow realization dawned on me, I can actually do this, by golly. I could actually turn this into a reality.

But it was still a dream, a fantasy, a pleasant daydream.

I read the ebook "The Trek" by David Schachne about his personal journey to EBC, which he in explicit, gory detail described as his personal "trip to hell." He was sick to the point of debilitation. He was freezing. He pushed himself to the point of utter exhaustion. And he never even made it to Everest Base Camp. (He did, though, make it to the top of Kala Patthar. More about that later.)

I had plenty of second thoughts about the feasibility of the trek but felt I could learn from his example of what "not" to do. Don't feast on the yak balls, for one. Seriously. Referring to spaghetti with meatballs, of course!

The lack of refrigeration on some points of the trail can make eating meat a hazardous activity.

I also gave more thoughts of how I could possibly keep myself warmer and not suffer through cold, sleepless nights and mornings.

But besides these trail-related issues, the real things holding me back were the real-world considerations that keep most of us tied tightly to the 8:00-5:00 world.

Could I get this hike done in a mere two weeks? What are all of my work mates going to think when I take off for another two (or more) weeks on top of all my other leave?

And what about mom? She is elderly and needs the support of all of her family. How can I think of leaving her for another two weeks on top of everything else?

There are plenty of other knickknack factors you can kick around in your head. Basic expenses are one. There are plenty of others. And health issues? That's a good reason to keep this in daydream mode.

You can literally die of altitude sickness on this trail. Everest Base Camp itself has an elevation of 17,598 feet. Kala Patthar, a popular mountain that is climbed to view Everest, is a stunning 18,200 feet high. At this altitude, the oxygen is at 50-percent compared to sea level. Just a bit scary!

Another issue one can banter about is age. But since I am in denial about such a concept, that wasn't a major issue for me personally.

All this being said, I got the idea of Everest stuck in my head. Viewing the videos, learning the names of the different towns along the way, started the process of making the trek more real. It wasn't this nebulous hike through the mountains. This was a trek from Lukla to Phakding (doable) to Namche Bazaar (doable), to Tengboche (doable), et cetera, until you reached EBC.

And then it happened one morning. I had the epiphany. It was about 4:00 a.m. It wasn't a workday, thank goodness. I woke up and sat up in bed. From the way I remember it, I woke up Thoy and announced, "I am going to Everest Base Camp."

She wasn't surprised by the announcement. She knows how I am. For being 4:00 a.m., she was actually quite supportive.

We actually got up out of bed and I took a moment to look in the mirror. Mid life, not in top physical condition, but I had not totally let myself go. I could do this. I was going to do this.

Probably.

And that is the whole concept of what I have been exploring so far. Had I pushed myself far enough to make this reality?

I talked to mom and explained that I planned to hike to EBC next fall, a bit over a year from now. It gave her plenty of time to get used to the idea. She was very supportive. I told her she could live vicariously through my adventure.

We read many of the same outdoor adventure books simultaneously, which gave us one more thing to bond over. In fact, she too read the book "The Trek" about David's personal EBC debacle.

On some level, though, I felt this was a cop-out. A year from now was feeling a bit "nebulous."

Soon thereafter, I was at the office and viewed the court schedule. Hmm. The schedule around Thanksgiving was a bit slower than usual. If I missed work during this two-week period, I would not burden my coworkers too much with my absence.

Hmm.

(By the way, I am an official court reporter in San Antonio, Texas working in federal court for the Honorable Xavier Rodriguez. If I take leave when court is in session, my fellow court reporters would have additional duties to take on besides their own court responsibilities.)

That's when epiphany number two hit. I could make this happen this year, in just a few months' time. And if I told my judge I was going, THAT would make this real. I would be too embarrassed to back out of this epic adventure after that. I could "trick myself" into making this real. As in real-real. All I had to do was tell him.

I took a deep breath and walked into his chambers. "Can I show you something real quick?"

"Sure. Come on in."

I pulled out my iPad and showed him my favorite pic of Namche Bazaar, with the beautiful snow-capped mountains in the background. It's a classic.

I explained I noted his schedule over the holidays and told him of my plans. He seemed reasonably impressed and gave me his blessings.

Now it was real. I couldn't - I wouldn't backtrack. I was going to Everest Base Camp - a dream trip of a lifetime.

And I felt I had tricked myself into making it real. On some level, I wasn't totally, 100-percent serious even when I asked for leave. On some level, it was still too big, too cold, too scary, too unknown, too far.

But once I made that announcement and got his blessing, I was committed - in a good way. I had made that transition from daydream to reality.

I was going to Everest Base Camp!

--*-*-*-*-*-*

Background

Even as a child, I was a frustrated climber. I remember going to Big Bend with my family while I was still quite the toddler and seeing this mound of rock and dirt about forty feet high. It's not that far from the camping/motel area by The Window. It had a pleasant slope, but just enough to make it look like "fun." I begged my father for permission to climb that small dirt hill, and he would have nothing to do with it. My father had a phobia when it came to heights, and all he could think of was having to "rescue" me from this small dirt mound.

Chatting at the office with Becky about this, she remembers this little hill from her own family trip to Big Bend. I was amazed. Of all the insignificant pile of rocks in the world, how could two people have such distinct, vivid memories of it?

I also remember distinctly driving back from Yosemite with my father on a family trip. When the roads got narrow and the drop-offs got steeper, he would shut his eyes tightly and cover them both with his hands. Thankfully, he wasn't driving at the time.

He just couldn't understand my attraction to the mountains. Even high overpasses on highways could give him the chills.

As soon as I got out of court reporting school and had a few dollars going jingle jangle in my pocket, I started organizing trips to Colorado car camping with my brother and friends.

I would bring along dinners I had made, put into plastic bags and frozen. I would fill up the ice chest and away we would

Early car camping expedition to Rocky Mountain National Park. David Anderson posing with "Dangerous Snow Field" sign with Ken Anderson (middle) and Joey Algier.

go. I remember many great day hikes we had at Rocky Mountain National Park, climbing high and sliding down the glaciers. Along the road, we would stop and play in the snowfields while the rangers yelled at us to get off of them, for some reason. Something to do with safety. We aptly ignored them until we were through with our snowball fights and glory photos.

One night I specifically remember was when Joe Algier joined our expedition to Colorado. (He was a family friend of Jerry Anderson, a court reporting friend I have known now for -- well, let's just say a few decades.). We were camping next to our truck at a privately run campground. I woke up in the morning and I noticed something sticking to the bottom part of my sleeping bag. It was Joey's leftover pizza. Sacrilege! That's not real camping, eating trailer park food! I was soooo disappointed in Joey.

But times and attitudes change. As the years went by, pizza became an integral part of our camping routine. Yosemite became our new destination of choice, and it was mandatory to order the veggie pizza at The Village either before or after hike climbing the 5,000-foot behemoth of a rock called Half Dome.

At age 23, I went on Outward Bound for 24 days in Washington state a few miles from the Canadian border. It was cold and wet. And I desperately missed my fiancé Lisa. We were actually able to receive mail during our hikes, ferried in by some trusted guide. I got a letter from Lisa saying she no longer wanted to get married. I can't remember the exact reasons. Something to do with the fact that she didn't love me anymore. I remember tramping through the mud and thinking, gosh, she could have waited until I got back from this trip to tell me that.

When I arrived in Fort Worth on my way back home to San Antonio, I was greeted with hugs and kisses from Lisa. I was a bit confused.

"I thought you wanted to break up."

"Oh, no. I was just in a bad mood that day," she said with the sincerest smile.

My picture in an Outward Bound brochure, Silver Leap Mountain, Washington State.

There were plenty of other dysfunctional relationships in the world to choose from -- and I did. Outward Bound, if nothing else, altered my life in that respect.

Another thing that Outward Bound did was it taught me dangerous mountaineering techniques. Or perhaps it would be more accurate to say it half taught me, which made me just smart enough to be dangerous.

One of the highlights of Outward Bound was finding some gigantic cliff to have us rappel off of. It made for glorious photo-ops and was good, clean fun.

Except it wasn't real rappelling-rappelling. We ran a single rope through the braking eight ring, while we were tied into a secondary rope and belayed by another mountaineering student. So we were double roped for insurance reasons.

What they didn't realize is that some of us might take what we learned here and apply it to real life. The first thing I did when I got home (besides dumping Lisa) was buy a 150-foot rope, dangle it off the cliff at Garner State Park and go over the edge with my eight ring as a braking mechanism.

As I was free-form dangling in space 150 feet up, my friends taking photos of me, I noticed something I had never noticed in the North Cascades - that a single rope through an eight ring has basically no friction in it. If I let go of the rope or slipped, I would slide down the rope at full speed, with the inevitable results following. I was basically Batman-ing down the rope, no differently as if I had no climbing gear at all.

I remember wrapping my foot around the rope slightly to give myself a bit more friction and was able to get down safely.

Next?

I joined the Alamo City Climbing Club and enjoyed this community during my late twenties and early thirties. This too was to change my life.

I met David Cain there, and together we had many a climbing adventure together, from Hueco Tanks near El Paso to the Pecos River Gorge near Del Rio to the top of Mount Rainier in Washington State.

But that wasn't the biggest way the ACCC changed my life.

David's brother, Reid Cain, taking a break near the top of Mount Rainier.

We had meetings once a month at Dang's Thai Restaurant on Austin Highway. A cute waitress by the name of Thoy was working evenings there, on top of her already full schedule at the University of Texas Health-Science Center.

I really wanted to ask her out, but I just couldn't build up the courage. I remember dialing the phone number of the restaurant before hanging up at the last second.

At the next meeting a month later, I got Thoy's attention for a moment and told her, "The last time I was here, I forgot something."

A concerned look came over her face. "Oh, what was that?"

"I forgot to tell you I would love to take you to dinner."

I don't think it was possible for her to have rolled her eyes any further back as she tilted her head to the heavens. I can still see it in slow motion. I knew I was shot down. I just knew it.

When her eyes came back down to meet mine, Thoy simply said, "Okay."

On the date number three, I told her, "I usually kiss a girl by the third date." She offered me her hand. "You can kiss my hand."

I was aghast. "I am not going to kiss your hand! I might bite it though!"

We got through the date. There was no biting. But I believe I did get a kiss good night.

And the rest is history.

Our first trip beyond Enchanted Rock north of San Antonio was Zion Canyon, where we climbed Angels Landing together. It is a thin fin of rock that climbs thousands of feet above the valley floor with cliff faces dropping away to all sides. At one point the trail narrows down to just a few feet, with sheer cliffs to both your left and right.

On my previous trip here, my water jug was bouncing around in the back of my pack, and I got a horrible attack of vertigo while crossing this. I immediately sat down on the rock ledge in front of me. The rock ledge may have been about six feet across, with the abyss falling away on both sides.

At the top of Half Dome, Yosemite National Park.

Thoy climbing the cables to the top of Half Dome.

I put my head between my knees to try to stop the spinning and to "keep the mountain from throwing me off." That's truly what it felt like. It was horrifying.

So I thought it was a perfect first climb for Thoy.

Thoy struggling through the Virgin River, "The Narrows," Zion Canyon National Park.

Thoy joined me on a number of adventures following that, believe it or not: hiking to the bottom of the Grand Canyon after a magnificent snowstorm, hiking The Narrows in Zion Canyon, and, of course, climbing Half Dome at Yosemite.

Thoy is not the tallest individual and this made The Narrows even more challenging. Miles of the trail is the actual Virgin River, IN the river. The walls of the canyon close in and for miles the river is the trail. There is no escape to either side. Which was no problem for myself, being about six feet tall. For Thoy, though, it was an epic battle of survival on the constant stream crossings, with the current threatening to sweep her away. I was constantly spotting her and giving guidance, sometimes to my own detriment. I was so distracted that twice I went completely underwater, backpack and all.

The Grand Canyon was memorable as the trail was coated with ice. We would just stand there and start sliding down the trail, often landing with a crash on our tailbones. No permanent damage done and we never went over the edge.

As the years went by, my hiking activities slowed down a bit. Thoy introduced me to her family in Thailand and many of our vacations centered around the Land of Smiles. My friend Eddie Fisher had invested in a number of condos along the beach and convinced me this was a reasonable thing to do. The price for one condo we found was extraordinarily reasonable. It was oceanfront on the sixteenth floor, less than $50,000, (just in case you are curious) and the association fees were about $12 a month. The condo was obtained.

And besides occasional drama, like broken water pipes in our absence, the property has worked out quite well for us. And somewhere along the way, mountain trips became secondary and relaxed beach time became the vacation of choice.

Thailand became a distraction from mountain trekking adventures for a number of years.

I never totally forgot the mountains. Eddie Fisher playing around during our trip to Valley of Fire State Park, Nevada.

Not that I totally forgot the mountains. Eddie and I would never go to Vegas without squeezing in a trip to Red Rocks or Valley of Fire. We even found a "fin" of rock that still sets off my vertigo every time we climbed it.

As I would try to crawl the last few feet to the narrowest section, it would feel as though the entire universe was closing in from all sides. It was a fascinating if not disorienting psychological adventure.

Just to give me additional heart palpitations. Eddie would do jumping jacks at the very top, with the abyss just a foot away on either side of him.

We would sit on top of this rock and take in the massive rock formations around us, trying to convince passing hikers down below to come join us. There were no takers. We would bake in the 100-plus degree heat until we were happily delirious, then climb back down.

And that pretty much brings us to the present.

I tell my son about my plans to go to Everest Base Camp. He quietly contemplates the concept.

He finally breaks the silence. "Dad, are you going through a midlife crisis?" He appears slightly concerned. He had become accustomed to the "chill-on-the-beach" version of his father.

I smile. "I don't think so. I have always been interested in such things."

In my mind, I am going to an alternate universe. I am going to the edge of the earth. I am going to peer over the edge and see what's there.

Why would anyone want to do anything else?

*_*_*_*_*_*_*_*

The Plan

There is a big map with a large expanse of blank space in the middle. That's how I felt about a large portion of the trek.

How is it all going to be filled in?

I started perusing trekking companies' web sites. Most of them listed an identical itinerary of 12 days, as follows:

Day 1. Fly into Lukla, then hike downhill to Phakding by the river.
Day 2. Hike uphill to Namche Bazaar.
Day 3. Acclimatization day in Namche Bazaar. Hike up to Everest View Lodge as a day hike.
Day 4. Hike to Tengboche.
Day 5. Hike to Dingboche.
Day 6. Acclimatization day in Dingboche.
Day 7. Hike to Lobuche.
Day 8. Hike to Gorak Shep and check into lodge. Day hike to EBC and back to Gorak Shep.
Day 9. Morning hike to the top of Kala Patthar, then hike to Pheriche.
Day 10. Hike to Namche Bazaar.
Day 11. Hike to Lukla.
Day 12. Fly back to Kathmandu.

Their pricing can be quite reasonable. My most recent perusal on the Internet showed prices starting at around $1,260 for a 14-day excursion. This includes the two days taken up flying into and out of Kathmandu, not listed above.

This price includes the flights to and from Lukla, guide and porter services, meals and lodging. Not a bad deal, considering the two flights coming and going to Lukla total around $300 and a personal porter guide hired on one's own would cost about $300.

Speaking somewhat in hindsight, an important consideration in hiring a trekking agency is that they will be of assistance in not only making your original reservations to Lukla and back but will assist in updating your flight schedule should there be weather-related delays.

The domestic terminal in Kathmandu and Lukla can be very unhappy places. Weather delays are common and competing with other frustrated Westerners to rebook canceled flights can be a very unpleasant and frustrating task.

There are some downsides to hiring a trekking service. One of these is you are expected to share a room with another trekker. I was not happy with this option. I wanted more personal space than that.

The lodges charge as little as $2 a night, so I think the issue here is just having a room available for all of the hikers. If you are traveling by yourself and thinking of using a trekking service, consider asking for the one-person-per-room upgrade.

These tours usually have a fixed dining menu, so some choices are given up there also.

And unless you are making arrangements for a large trekking group, the lodges you stay in will also be preset. All lodges are not created equal. Not all lodges have identical amenities.

Another possible downside (not necessarily, mind you) is the group you are going with. You know how people can be. You may be a millennial stuck with a delegation from Generation X. You may be a Gen Xer stuck with a bunch of millennials.

All that being said, hiring a trekking agency takes care of a lot of unknowns. There is nothing wrong with this option, but it's not the one I chose.

*_*_*_*_*_*_*_*

I was looking for a more independent path, but I still wanted some guidance and assistance, especially when it came to carrying my pack.

Scouring the Internet for data, I read the trip report of a couple from India that had hired a guide named Chhiring Sherpa. The article included his phone number and I attempted to give him a call.

The phone rang and the dial tone sounded very far away. It appeared someone answered on the other end, but it was barely audible. No meaningful communication was had.

A day or two later, I got a text from this number asking if I had called. I responded that I had, texting Chhiring that I was looking for a guide to Everest Base Camp.

He then asked me a very interesting question. "Do you want just a guide or a porter-guide?"

Chhiring went on to inform me that if I just wanted a guide, the cost would be $20 a day. If I wanted a porter-guide, that is, for him to carry my backpack, the cost would be $25 a day. I was somewhat entertained by this choice. For me, it wasn't a choice at all.

The plan was to hike above 17,000 feet. The air is thin up there.

"I want a porter-guide."

During my trek, I would only see one situation where a Westerner was carrying his own heavy backpack with a guide at his side carrying a small daypack.

The guide had a certain smile on his face, which I interpreted as, yes, this crazy Westerner is saving $5 a day.

*_*_*_*_*_*_*_*

Preparation

"Where the heck is my backpack?"

The last time I had used my backpack was on a 2008 trip to Yosemite with my buddy Jerry six years previously. We had camped near North Dome high on a ridge with a great view of Half Dome. I remember it was a cold night but I slept like a baby in my massive sleeping bag. Jerry shivered all night long. I had meant to warn him about those K Mart specials.

I had gone top to bottom in my house and garage a number of times and just couldn't put my finger on it. I was confident no one broke in and stole only my backpack, so I knew it was here...somewhere.

I finally found it in the garage inside a plastic bag that I had earlier mistaken for my son's roly-poly back massager. That's the best I can describe it. It's one of those things that eventually winds up in the garage.

I then pulled my sleeping bag off the top shelf of the bedroom closet and started jamming it in the backpack. My gosh, I didn't remember it was this big. I weighed the sleeping bag and it came in at over six pounds. With the pack, I was over ten pounds and I hadn't even gotten started.

Sometimes with time, things get smaller. Sometimes they get bigger. Sometimes things just get heavier. I was a bit taken aback by this beginning process. Without a stuff sack, the sleeping bag took up practically the entire backpack. This just wasn't going to work.

Packing for a camping trip is always a balancing act. There's a constant battle between weight and necessity. Well, if not necessity, then the desire for a few creature comforts, like food.

I was already losing the balancing act and was falling off the high wire.

Thoy was monitoring my progress in the living room. It was beginning to look cluttered with bits of gear scattered about the room. There was need for adult supervision. She stood beside me as I pulled the sleeping bag from the backpack and dug into the bottom of the pack. I began pulling out a few indiscriminate items.

Some of these indiscriminate items happened to be a handful of Magnum condoms.

Thoy gave me a perplexed look. I gave myself a perplexed look.

The last time I had used the backpack was on my trip to Yosemite.

"Gosh, I must have been thinking really positively on my last trip with Jerry." I gave a weak chuckle.

Thoy suddenly became a bit more intrigued with my packing activities.

A bit befuddled, I continued to pull out detritus from the pack. Next I pulled out a colorful brochure. At first, I thought it was from a city in California.

It happened to be from Wellington, New Zealand. Which, conveniently, I have never been to. And then the heavens opened and a revelation came to me. My son had borrowed the backpack for his month-long trip to New Zealand. Which was even more convenient.

Case closed, Sherlock Holmes!

I continued to examine the backpack and noticed a powdery, sticky substance along a large portion of the inside of the backpack.

Did someone (a/k/a my son) spill lemonade mix or the like into my pack? Well, that little heathen!

Repeated attempts to clean the substance had little effect. What is this stuff?

After putting on my reading glasses, it became apparent the pack's weather coating had started to disintegrate. An unending abundance of sticky flakes was constantly shedding and sticking to whatever was inside the pack, be it sleeping bag, clothes, food or electronics.

Maybe I am just prissy. Or maybe that is just gross. I am leaning toward the conclusion that it is just gross. I wasn't happy about it. There were enough unknowns I was going to encounter. I just didn't want sticky bits of plastic in my hair, on my clothes and who knows where else in the depths of the mountains of Nepal.

Deep sigh.

Evidently, this happens with backpacks of indeterminate age

stored in the back of garages. That being said, I hadn't used the backpack that many times. It looked brand new on the outside.

The good news is that REI has a lifetime warranty on their backpacks. I took the backpack to the local REI store. I was very courteously informed that, well, no, lifetime doesn't really mean lifetime. This was not covered by their warranty. But it didn't hurt to ask.

The realization was slowly coming to me that I needed to do some serious shopping.

It was time to get a new backpack.

And my old sleeping bag, six pounds? Are you kidding me? Six pounds? That's ridiculous. No wonder I was warm on North Dome!

Time for a new sleeping bag.

And the list continued and spiraled out of control.

The bottom line, I was emerging from a years-long hibernation from backpacking, and it was just that time in the life cycle to do some serious shopping.

Hiking shoes. The whole technology of hiking shoes has evolved to a level that even ancient space aliens would marvel at. My last pair of hard, stiff, unyielding leather hiking boots was guaranteed to give you countless blisters, pain and misery.

"Oh, but they provide great ankle support." This is the universal hiking wisdom never questioned over the decades.

And the corresponding reassurance was also given to the masses: "Don't worry. They will break in." Sure, they would, eventually. Maybe after a few years.
My life experience has taught me that promised day of nirvana never comes.

But this is a new age. The new lighter, kinder hiking boots are downright dreamy. In fact, they don't appear to be designed by a sadist with a foot fetish.

They are kind of like glorified tennis shoes with a higher top for at least the appearance of ankle support.

And with every piece of gear, there are decisions to be made. Whole forums are devoted to the pros and cons of different types of clothing and gear for backpacking. It is a world unto itself.

And information is good. Right? Truth is good. Choices are good. Independent thinking is bad. Wait. Or is it good? Being part of the Borg collective is bad. At least according to Captain Picard. We can trust Captain Picard, right? If we can't trust Captain Picard --

Wait, wait, wait! What am I talking about? Just stop! Stop! Stay on point!

And similar to the above mish-mash of ideas and concepts, among all this goodness of information and truth came a dark cloud of confusion. Every piece of gear came with multiple strengths and weaknesses. A wrong choice was going to have consequences that could drastically affect my trip. It could end my trip. For days, I felt paralyzed with indecision. Where do I start? Where do I end?

What if I don't take enough supplies? What if I take too much? Can I get last-minute supplies in Lukla? In Namche Bazaar?

I wasn't happy with my fuzzy mental state and made a renewed effort to get organized. I would focus on one thing at a time. How about start from the bottom and work up? Socks. That should be easy.

Well, what kind of socks? Polypropylene? Wool? Cotton? Thick or thin?

Polypropylene wicks away moisture. Wool is warm but heavier. Cotton is soft and comforting. They also take a long time to dry and can get stinky.

How many pair of wool socks? Polypropylene? Cotton? Should I bring along some of each just to be sure? What kind of socks are best at preventing blisters?

How are these thick wool socks going to affect the size of the hiking boots I buy? Can I fit this all in my pack?

Hindsight note 1: I wound up wearing polypropylene base-layer socks with a thick wool sock on top of this. This was very comfortable and I never got a single blister during the trek, which was quite surprising to me. I also brought along a pair of cotton socks, but I never used them during the trek.

And while we are still dealing with footwear, what brand of hiking shoes? What size? How tight should they feel when I am trying them on at Whole Earth Provisions? Are they too heavy? Are they too light and not providing enough ankle support? Are they waterproof? Water-resistant? Do I

34

really want to spend $200 on these things?

Do I even need hiking boots? I had gotten in the habit of just wearing tennis shoes on my trips to Yosemite. They had worked out just fine. Along with hiking shoes, how about bringing along a backup pair of tennis shoes to wear around the lodge? Good grief. How about flip flops?

The decision was made to take hiking boots only, along with a pair of flip flops.

Hindsight note 2: The flip flops were probably excessive but wound up being very much appreciated for quick trips to the bathroom in the middle of the night.

Working my way up, I purchased a new pair of hiking pants, along with a wind shell to go over them.

Hindsight note 3: I never used the wind shell pants. I also never used the pair of shorts I brought along.

What about underwear? There is a lot of new technology out there. I thought it was necessary to buy some Underarmour underwear. But I am set in my ways. I didn't like the fit and was just as happy with my regular cotton briefs.

There was one more thing to think of before I got up above the waist and that was thermal underwear.

Hindsight note 4: Merino wool underwear was the best investment I made for the trip.

"Well, isn't it itchy?" my friend asked me.

No, it's not. It's as smooth as cashmere, or at least what I would envision cashmere to be like.

The price was around $70 for tops and another $70 for the bottoms. I thought the salesman at REI was just trying to make a sale. No. All of the wonderful qualities you might hear about merino wool are true.

It is soft, comforting and warm. Merino wool also doesn't absorb odor like polyester and cotton. This was my luxury item when I left the lodges to go to my cold, dark room and crawl into my sleeping bag. I only wore it at nighttime so it was reasonably clean against my skin during the night. (Others wear it all day long.) Merino wool helped keep me sane. I even wore it on the plane ride home after the trip. It was the cleanest smelling thing I had.

Shirts? Cotton? Polyester? Cotton is softer on the skin. Polyester is lighter and doesn't hold onto moisture like cotton. How about some of both?

Hindsight note 5: Your cotton and polyester are going to stink to high heaven by the end of this trip. Some hikers have a wash-as-you-go routine, but I found it too cold for my clothes to dry in an appropriate amount of time. For my next hiking trip, I actually added more merino wool to the mix and less cotton and polyester.

Add to all of this a fleece jacket, a soft-shell jacket, a down coat and wind shell. Stuff, stuff, stuff into that backpack! I just couldn't decide between the fleece jacket and the soft-shell, so I took both. I know that's excessive.

Hindsight note 6: On my next extended hiking trip, I opted

on the soft-shell jacket and left the fleece jacket at home.

That being said, the fleece is softer and more comforting. I enjoyed wearing it when I would initially crawl into my sleeping bag at night. But the tighter fabric of the soft-shell keeps a lot of the wind off in moderate conditions. In the mid stages of this hike, you will experience temperature swings from sweating to shivering as you move in and out of the shade and wind. The soft-shell is best for the shivering, windy portions of the hike.

Hindsight note 7: I had so many layers laying on my floor before the trip, I was considering not taking the down coat. That would not have been a good idea. In South Texas, it is easy to forget about the concept of "cold" until it is too late.

And then there was electronic gadgetry. I bought a Go Pro. I bought an altimeter with a temperature gauge. I already had a digital camera and iPad that I brought along.

Hindsight note 8: I never used the Go Pro on the trip and this was added weight I could have lived without, since it was a permanent resident in my daypack. The altimeter was a great addition. It added a lot of enjoyment to the trip, keeping track of one's progress up and down the mountains. I was also quite interested in checking the thermometer in the morning to see just how cold it was outside of my sleeping bag.

I added a number of food items to the packing list. Nuts, trail mix, beef jerky, granola bars, coconut bars, craisins. That's all I will confess to now.

In the past, I had usually erred on the side of too much

weight, and this carried over into this trip. It is just my basic nature. I can't help it. I took a hardback Stephen King novel on one trip to the top of Half Dome. Another time, I took Jon Krakauer's "Into Thin Air." It seemed like the appropriate thing to do at the time.

Then there is that special moment before the big trip. You have your gear and clothing scattered out on the living room floor. Your backpack lies empty. The time comes to stuff what you can stuff into the backpack and the rest is left behind.

Time solves all problems. Time forces us to make the best choices we are capable of making.

The backpack is full and it's time to go to the Himalayas.

--*-*-*-*-*-*

Day 1 – Flight toward Lukla

Although my initial flight segment left on Friday, November 14, 2014, I have always considered "Day 1" to be when I actually arrived in Nepal. In my mind, that is when the trip actually began. From the time I began my journal on the trail and throughout the extensive editing process that followed, I have always organized my journal numerically by day from that point forward.

To me, "Day 1" will always be Sunday, November 16, 2014.

--*-*-*-*-*-*

The flight segments took me from San Antonio to Houston, Houston to Vancouver, then Vancouver to Istanbul.

All of these flights were directly on schedule all the way to Istanbul. But once arriving there and looking at the departure board, there was one flight showing a four-hour delay, and that was my flight to Kathmandu.

Originally scheduled to land at 7:30 a.m. Sunday morning in Kathmandu, I was now officially going to miss my 10:30 a.m. flight to the mountain town of Lukla.

Would it be possible to get a flight later in the day? That was the only way I would be able to stay on schedule.

I kept my eye on the departure board just in case they canceled the delay (which can happen), but no such luck. I now had a ten-hour layover with my flight leaving on early Sunday morning at 12:30 a.m.

I drift to sleep off and on, so I set my alarm to make sure I don't miss my flight.

I am able to contact Chhiring Sherpa by text and tell him of my delay. He is waiting for me in Lukla already. He is a bit confused of why I am not in the country already.

As the plane gets closer to Kathmandu, there is a majestic view of the Himalayan range. I am inspired and intrigued.

I notice our plane is going in circles. Far below, I see another jetliner doing the same.

Fog in Kathmandu was holding things up. A delayed flight into Kathmandu and now fog. These are not good portents.

We start our approach to Kathmandu and go over the mountains from the south. Many of the mountaintops were flattened for cultivation with little farmhouses nearby. Very scenic, very cool-looking. I am trying to take it easy on superlative adjectives at this point.

As we get closer to town, apartment-style buildings are separated by small parcels of cultivated land. Then there are just apartment-style buildings. Lots of them. Many appear much older than others. The view reminds me of something out of a Star Wars movie. I had never seen anything like this. It was surreal.

We land and I head through immigration. After getting in the right line, (you need to get in line one before line two right next to it), I have my tourist visa issued. The clerk hands me my paperwork.

I am told gruffly, "We are finished. Walk!"

I head toward baggage claim and things start to get congested. The gentleman behind me violates my personal space so I start massaging his big belly with my elbow. He doesn't seem to mind.

There is actually a metal detector at the entrance to the baggage claim area and I start to grab a basket to put my phone in. "No! Go!" The alarm buzzes as I walk through and they wave me on.

Our flight is not even on the display boards so I prepare for a wait. A few flights from the region have just previously landed.

I see my duffel bag come down the conveyor in a reasonable amount of time and I feel like I just hit the jackpot.

I can't find any carts so I carry my 40-pound duffel bag along with everything else. It's heavy.

Hitting the front of the airport I look for the Tara Airlines domestic flight area and I immediately get hit by all the touts, one young man in particular.

"No more flights to Lukla today, but I can take you to hotel." I just didn't like him. It was like I've had this conversation before.

I start asking around and an older gentleman offers to lead the way to the domestic terminal.

The older man tells me, "They are liars. Maybe we can get

you a flight." The young man continues to follow us.

"Sir, I can -- blah blah blah."

I just wasn't in the mood. I turn to the young man. "Don't even talk to me!"

"Excuse me?"

"I am already being helped."

Note: Please don't think anything too negatively of me and certainly not the people of Nepal because of this interaction. Airport touts do NOT represent a country's culture.

The domestic terminal was much farther than I expected. It was an entirely different area of the complex. The older gentleman suggested a cart to put my duffel bag on. Brilliant idea!

We push the cart down the roadway, then drag it up a dirt embankment and we are there.

We are met by his friend, who looks just a bit sketchy. He tells us all flights to Lukla are indeed canceled for the day. Everything I hear I am taking with a grain of salt. My fraud radar is at full alert, but still, my gut tells me to believe him. Kind of. Maybe.

It is foggy out and most flights leave in the morning. It made sense.

"But there is good news, my friend!"

He tells me there is one spot left on a helicopter leaving in a few hours.

After reading so many trip reports of people being stuck in the terminal for days, I was willing to consider this option. "How much?"

"$400."

My head was whirring with all the possibilities. There was a chance I would give this fellow $400 and I would never see him again. There was a chance I would get stuck in this airport for days and be out $400.

Mental calculations were made. The computational device in my head whirred, spun and sputtered, in danger of overheating.

I decided to err on the side of possibly being scammed. It was kind of disconcerting.

I didn't know what the "rules" were. Who could I believe and who couldn't I believe?

Inside the terminal I go to the helicopter counter and they start preparing a ticket for me. Okay. I feel a bit better.

I go over to the Tara counter and notice the large sign announcing "All flights to Lukla delayed due to fog." I feel like maybe I did the right thing.

The PA system announces, "All flights to Lukla are canceled for the day. Please report to the ticket counter." As this just applied to the airplane schedule, I began feeling like I was very lucky indeed!

We are scheduled to leave at 1:00 and shortly thereafter we are escorted to a truck where we get in and wait. Then we are told to get back out and wait in the terminal again.

"There is a substantial delay."

"Substantial?" That's a mighty big word to be using.

I ask, "Are we going to get there today?"

The guide says, "I hope so."

We return inside and just a few minutes later we are told to go back to the truck. Cool!

We drive down and around the edges of the airport to the helicopter pad and wait for about 20 minutes for them to prepare and figure out how to load our cargo.

And off we go! This was my first helicopter ride. I could feel the powerful force of the thrust as we lift off. Very exciting!

We zip over the city landscape before heading into the mountains. We skirt mountain walls and barely swing over mountain passes on our way in. This is all done very carefully, as it is still quite foggy.

We make a landing on a small flat piece of earth on the side of a mountain next to a quaint teahouse. It's the only structure in the area.

"Is this Lukla?"

"No, this is not Lukla. Lukla is at top of mountain."

Oh, geez. The helicopter starts to take off and I motion, "I don't have one of my bags!" The guide points to the other side of the helicopter where they placed it on the ground. Whew!

I get my thoughts together and ask, "Where are we?"

"We are in Surkye." Something like that. I don't have a clue.

"Where is Lukla?"

"Five hundred meters up over that hill."

Oh, goodness. I had gear I planned to stash at Lukla. I had not planned on carrying this up 1,500 feet late in the day with dark coming! By myself!

All that being said, this was an absolutely lovely little spot in the mountains.

I asked the other group's guide if he could call my Sherpa guide, so he could tell him exactly where I was. We all agreed it would be wise for him to come here.

While he was doing that, I sent Chhiring Sherpa a text. It would not go through. No signal.

The guide came back and told me the same thing. "Sorry. No signal. I cannot reach him either."

Deep sigh.

*_*_*_*_*_*_*_*

Pemba, the other group's guide, had arranged for porters to run to Surkye, if that's where we were. Rob, Mark and his girlfriend Sam would just carry daypacks and I knew I couldn't keep up with them with all my gear. No way.

Pemba and I compared numbers again, confirmed it was correct, and he tried to call Chhiring again. He eventually got through and Chhiring was on his way to help me out.

Since I could relax a bit now I went inside to order my first bowl of noodle soup in Nepal. The rest of the group was almost finished with theirs. I just couldn't relax enough to eat until I figured out the situation.

The lady of the establishment went out to pick fresh greens from the garden and went to work.

Still a bit reticent about getting sick, (the Internet is great about keeping you informed of such things) I asked her to make it extra hot.

"Uh, not spicy hot. The other kind of hot." Pemba laughed. He knew what I was saying.

I went back outside as porters came running down the hill and started loading up. They were in a hurry. This was not a part of their itinerary to run down here to retrieve these hikers. They quickly threw the packs onto their back and rapidly scampered back up the hill.

Soon, the rest of the group was gone and it started getting lonely.

I wondered when they knew about the change of plans. Was it even before we left Kathmandu? Did everybody know about the itinerary change but me?

Evidently. How else could the porters have gotten there that quickly?

A ten-year-old girl, whose grandfather worked on the property, along with her nine-year-old brother, overcame their shyness and started talking to me. Her English was extraordinarily good.

They showed off their climbing skills on a nearby bluff and did cartwheels in the field.

Landing pad and play area in the Khumbu.

Then they stacked up a number of symmetrically rounded rocks one directly on top of the other and started throwing other rocks at the pile to try to knock it down. It looked like great fun. They offered me a rock to give it my best shot. I missed by just a tad. About three feet.

Hey, I could market this concept in Amerca! I'm going to be rich! And just balance your mate's beer on a competing second stack of rocks to up the ante. The possibilities were endless!

I had quite a bit of time to take in my new surroundings. The small residence had beautiful rockwork on their front patio. The air was crisp and cool. The view was fantastical. The mountainside was steep, with the valley far below. The valley receded endlessly to the south, the direction we had come by helicopter.

The children played nearby. An elderly woman hauled loads of yak dung, storing it for future fertilization or fuel. She was all smiles as I snapped a photo of her walking by. She was all business, though, and never thought to stop and pose.

A cultivated field was directly behind the residence. Dried corncobs were stacked symmetrically in bins next to the field. There was a small, flat "play area" in front of the lodge before the precipitous drop to the valley.

The ambiance was that of a tranquil Tolkienesque Hobbit burrow. I was completely enthralled.

Had my journey ended at that moment, the entire trip would have still been worthwhile.

--*-*-*-*-*-*

Two hours after Pemba was able to contact Chhiring, he showed up. I was very happy to see him. He was sweating profusely. He had been running and walking the past two hours from Lukla to Surkye and had initially gone to the wrong heli pad.

"You told me 1:00 at Lukla."

I smiled. "Yes. That's exactly what I told you."

He smiled and nodded. The concept of the best-laid plans going awry was universal.

By then, I had already taken the backpack out of the duffel bag and started to organize things. Inside the duffel bag next to the backpack was my brand-new down jacket. It didn't "quite yet" fit inside the backpack, but scrunched up quite nicely next to it in the duffel bag.

I had also taken a carry-on satchel onto the plane with "stuff" I had planned on leaving in Lukla.

This too was dumped into the duffel bag.

Research (i.e., surfing the Internet) had indicated the lodges didn't mind leaving gear behind at their locale, as it helped guarantee they would have a return customer after the client's hike.

In hindsight – and, as my son would say, even with foresight – it was evident I had taken a bit too much in the way of supplies.

Doesn't everyone bring jars of almond butter and picante sauce in their backpack? No? Okay. Point taken. I will do better next time.

Chhiring took the backpack. I took the duffel bag. The
duffel bag was lighter.

We got underway. Chhiring said he knew a "shortcut" so we
could bypass Lukla and get closer to Phakding, our original
goal of the day. Plus we wouldn't have to climb quite so
high before heading back down.

Brilliant idea!

We got to hiking for a while and I asked, "Are we going to
be hiking in the dark?"

"Yes."

And we started hiking uphill. Quite a bit. After a while, I
cried uncle and let him carry just a bit more of the combined
gear. In return, I carried his pack, which weighed about one
kilo. Amazing!

Ever so often, I would say, "Quick break." Actually, I said it
quite a bit. I think it was going to become my favorite
phrase of the trip.

I started sweating through my soft-shell jacket and started
hiking in short sleeves.

The duffel bag was clunky on my back, as it wasn't
designed for hiking. The straps were too long. I tried to
compensate for the long straps by pulling them closer to the
center of my chest. This made it fit better and not be so
floppy.

It was getting pretty dark and I was walking on the left-hand side of the trail, adjusting the duffel bag, as usual. I looked through a few plants and noticed I was walking about one foot from the precipice falling away hundreds of feet to the river below. It was a bit startling.

Karl, you really need to pay attention! It would have been very embarrassing to end the trek on day one.

We crossed our first suspension bridge, which was pretty cool. Bouncy bouncy! I could still see the outline of the waterfall and river running beneath us.

It became officially dark and with the cloud cover there would be no help from the stars or moon.

Chhiring asked, "Do you have a flashlight?"

"Uh, no. How about you?"

Chhiring shook his head sideways.

I was embarrassed. Out of all the gear I had packed, with all of the planning I had done, how could I forget a stupid flashlight?

This wasn't the first time I had put myself in this type of situation.

--*-*-*-*-*-*

In my early twenties, I made my first trip to Yosemite and caught my first glimpse of the enigmatic Half Dome. From the valley floor, it rises 5,000 feet directly above you. It's a sight you don't forget.

The desire to be on top of this magnificent dome was overwhelming. Unfortunately, this was just a quick day trip. I had been hired as a court reporter to take depositions in San Francisco and I had to get right back to town. But I made immediate plans to return.

Hiking in the dark with Chhiring.

Soon thereafter, I flew from San Antonio into Oakland and drove late into the night toward Yosemite. I checked into a motel halfway there, leaving the rest of the drive for the next morning.

I arrived at Yosemite at about 1:00 the next afternoon, and there was Half Dome waiting for me.

I had planned to do the 20-mile trek starting the next day after getting a backpacking permit. But instead, I got a case of summit fever and decided I would just "day hike" it that afternoon.

It wasn't a rational decision. I threw my water bottle, a few granola bars and topo maps into my daypack and took off.

The hike to the top of Half Dome is epic. The first section follows next to the Merced River, including two magnificent waterfalls and the tumultuous rapids inbetween. The river is then left behind for further climbing toward the ridge overlooking the valley floor. The dome proper is then encountered, with steep stone steps cut into the mountain. Finally, it is necessary to pull oneself up a cable for the last 350 feet.

And then I was on the top of Half Dome, standing on the edge, looking down at the valley 5,000 feet below. I was ecstatic.

It was now about 8:00 o'clock at night and I began considering my options. I was thinking of spending the night on the top of the dome, even though I was just in shorts and a t-shirt. I could just park on that rock over there. That would be really cool, I thought.

I started a conversation with another hiker and started considering the reality of this.

"Do you think it's going to get cold tonight?" He indicated it would.

Oh, crap. I had never considered that. I had seen the movie "Rambo" where Rambo hid in a mountain stream while the military was looking for him. He seemed to be okay. It's just mind over matter, right?

Yes, it is, in the movies. Living in San Antonio, I had forgotten about the concept of cold. I decided I should try to make my way back down the mountain as quickly as possible.

I literally slid down the side of the dome on the cable section and was making great time. I made it all the way back down to the Merced River before I lost my way in the dark.

Did I mention I didn't have a flashlight with me?

I was close to the river on a rock ledge and wasn't sure where the trail went from there. I could hear the roar of the river just a stone's throw away. I decided to call it a night. I pulled out my topo maps and tried to make them into a blanket. It didn't work out very well.

After a while, I got cold and decided to backtrack to see what I could figure out. Maybe something serendipitous would happen.

After hiking another mile or so in the dark I saw a campfire in the distance and made my way toward it. There were a couple of young female campers by a campfire and they were gracious enough to let me warm up by the fire.

After a bit of small talk, and a bit of chastisement for my lack of preparedness, they got ready to turn in for the evening.

"Do you mind if I stay here by the fire? I will be just fine."

"Don't be ridiculous. You can share a sleeping bag with us."

I was dumbfounded by their generosity. And I did not succumb from hypothermia that night and lived to tell the tale.

And as I stumbled through the dark in the Himalayas, I scolded myself again for the lack of preparedness. How could I be so foolish?

And the possible answer came to me in the form of a question. Do I have some type of Freudian compulsion to getting lost in the dark?

Who's to say? I just hope it's not the death of me one day.

--*-*-*-*-*-*

Chhiring dug into his one-kilo knapsack and pulled out his iPhone. He then activated flashlight mode and we continued to hike through the night. I made more of an effort to stay on the mountain side of the trail versus the cliff side.

I told Chhiring how in America when parents take their kids on long road trips, they constantly call out, "Are we almost there?" He laughed.

"Yes. Bad guide say five minutes, then ten minutes, then 15 minutes."

A bit further into the night I asked for the first time on the trip, but certainly not the last, "How much further?"

"About 45 more minutes." I was getting tired.

At every light of every small residence, I would ask, "Is this it?"

"Just around the corner."

We finally arrived at our destination for the evening. I stayed on the trail as Chhiring went through a gate, up a few stairs to a small lodge on the side of the mountain. The lodge is quite dark with no apparent activity. Chhiring knocks on the door. No answer. He walks over to a window, raps on it and finally gets a response.

A father and his son are inside and we are the only guests for the evening. They already have a wood fire burning in the stove in the corner of the lodge.

I ask Chhiring what time it is.

He shows me his watch. It was only 6:30 o'clock.

I am shocked. What? In the morning? I had thought it was at least 8:00.

It gets dark extremely early this time of year, evidently.

Chhiring asks if I want something to drink.

I tell him iced water. He laughs. I am not sure if it was the "iced" part or not.

I know I must have misheard him. "We do not have water here." He goes to a high shelf and starts shuffling and looking behind the beer and sodas on the shelf.

"Ah, one water left for you!" It was a larger liter bottle and that was good. I hadn't thought to bring water along on the trek. After all, I was going to land in Lukla.

We get situated and I order fried potatoes and mushroom soup. The son adds a bit more wood to the small stove and starts meal preparation.

"Are you going to eat, Chhiring?"

The lodge owner's son helps prepare dinner.

"Later."

In just a bit I am brought my steaming, giant, massive plate of potatoes. I tell Chhiring there is no way I can eat all of it and offer to share. He accepts my offer and they bring another plate.

We also end up splitting the mushroom soup, and the older gentleman "tops off" my soup with what is left in the pot.

"So this is called a tea house?"

"No, this is a lodge. Tea houses just provide food and drink along the way."

He informs me many of the structures we passed earlier were "porter houses," where porters stay. The way I was feeling along the hike, they looked just fine to me.

I was curious to see my room so the lodge owner, Chirring and myself go up the stairs and they show me my basic room. It had a window and two beds, with wood floors, walls and ceiling. It even had an electric light!

It would do quite nicely.

"Where are the room numbers?"

Even the lodge owner laughed. "Not necessary. Only five rooms."

Chhiring informed me there were two kinds of toilets available, guest toilets and porter toilets. He gave me the grand tour. Ducking our heads, we walked through a small doorway into an unlighted room. In the middle of the floor was a squat toilet.

"And this is the guest toilet?"

"Yes."

Then he described the porter toilet, which involved leaves and eventual composting.

I tell Chhiring I am turning in early. I go upstairs and start sorting my gear. Eventually, he comes back upstairs to check on me and I start showing him my gear.

"If you are going to have to carry this stuff, you might as well know what it is."

I show him my clothes, the rest of my "gear" sheepishly and guiltily explain a lot of the weight is food. Maybe bringing the Pace picante sauce was a bit excessive.

He approves of my clothes selection and I offer him the picante sauce as my personal guilt offering. He unwraps the plastic I have it wrapped in and seems quite interested.

"Oh, pickled!" His family lives in Namche, tomorrow's goal/destination, and I tell him he can take it there if he likes.

I lay out my sleeping bag on the bed, with a cloth liner inside. I put on my merino wool base and my fleece jacket. I crawl inside and get quite comfy.

What am I forgetting? Oh, yes. The nice THICK blanket they brought up to the room. I retrieve it from the other bed, lay it over the top of my sleeping bag and settle back in.

I am warm and feeling quite good about the day's adventures. I go to sleep with a dumb grin on my face.

--*-*-*-*-*-*

Journal entry from early morning hours of Day 2:

I wake up feeling quite refreshed at some point in the night feeling toasty warm. I take off my fleece jacket, my wool bottoms and kick off the blanket.

I am just laying there, noticing a portion of the wood on the ceiling looks like a fat penguin. I might as well get up for a while.

I pull out my iPad to check the time. 10:00 o'clock?? No way! Then I remember that is still reflecting Istanbul time. I try to do the math and figure it is "maybe" 3:00 in the morning.

I am awake so I decide to work on my journal a bit.

After working on my journal into the early morning hours, I notice it is 12:05 Istanbul time and my iPad is down to 61-percent charged. Hopefully I can recharge it in Namche.

I am actually able to get back to sleep for a while. I wake up with the sun shining at about 7:40.

To be continued.

--*-*-*-*-*-*

Day 2 – Hike to Namche Bazaar

"I can barely remember this morning. It was a long time ago." First journal entry for day two.

--*-*-*-*-*-*

November 17, 2014.

It was very exciting to wake up the next morning and be able to take in my surroundings. The sun was shining and the day was full of possibilities.

The valley fell away to the south and majestic mountains soared to the north.

This is the magnificent view from outside Danfe Lodge. What a great way to start the day!

The Danfe Lodge has a small, flat yard in front of it with a garden, with bins of cornhusks on the edge, just like at the teahouse where we had landed the day before.

I wasn't exactly sure where we were, but we had not yet reached the trail that led from Lukla to Phakding. We were still "off route." But we had hiked late into the night – or so it seemed – so we couldn't be that far away.

To have been on schedule the day before, we would have made it from Lukla to Phakding, a somewhat leisurely walk mostly downhill to the river.

To get back on schedule today, all we had to do was reach Phakding and then tackle the steep uphill climb to Namche. No problem!

I still have extra gear that is not necessary for the hike and I discuss the situation with Chhiring. Leaving it at Danfe Lodge is not a good option, as we don't plan to come back to this location – wherever we are. Chhiring suggests offering the lodge owner's son $5 to take it to Lukla. Deal! Good kid!

I carefully go through my things and fill up my carry-on to give to the young man. It was a great weight off of my shoulders in terms of backpacker guilt. It was a great weight off of Chhiring's shoulders in terms of weight.

I order the chapati and eggs for breakfast. And just like the night before, it was prepared over the wood stove in the corner. Which, in and of itself, at some basic, primordial level in my psyche, was so comforting and reassuring.

It transported me back to a simpler time, a time even before my own recollection. It transported me back to my mother's stories, where she and her siblings would sit around the wood-burning stove during the winter. Mom told me how it was necessary to call out "save" if you left your spot or you would lose your prime seating.

Perhaps it transported me back even further, to ancestral memories of a warming fire that the tribe would gather around, telling their stories, passing on their traditions and cooking their meals. It felt like a simple goodness for the soul. I wasn't in Kansas anymore. I wasn't ordering a Happy Meal. This was the polar opposite of modern society. It felt simple and good.

Segueing back to breakfast, chapati is basically like a big flour tortilla. Being from Texas, I wound up making a big, giant taco out of it. Yum! But it definitely could have used some salsa that I had already given to Chhiring. Plus some napkins.

I order the Sherpa tea Chhiring is drinking. He tells me they put salt, butter and milk in it. Although it makes sense to have more fat in your diet at higher altitudes, the concept of buttery tea was a bit too much. My mind just couldn't find a place to categorize the taste and I had to fight back the gag reflex. I am not a picky person. I will eat and drink just about anything, a lot like Mikey, but this was a struggle.

Trying to be a good guest, I am almost able to finish my cup and, ever so graciously, the attentive lodge owner immediately fills it back to the rim.

After breakfast, I organize my pack and am ready to go. I feel good. I am ready to rock'n'roll.

The lodge owner brings over the ledger and I have a mental drum roll in my head for the grand tally. It was around $12, $13. Two dollars of this was for the room. A large portion of this was for the soda that Chhiring had the night before and my liter of water, which had to be carried in by porter, mule or yak. The remainder was for the evening and morning meals.

We walk down the path a few hundred yards and I realize something is missing. My hiking pole! Argh! Chhiring is gracious enough to run back and get it. I again feel guilt mixed with gratitude.

I am already deep in his debt, way beyond the nominal fee he is charging.

While waiting, I pull out my iPad and make a few notes in my journal. A group of young girls that are heading to school stop by to check out the Westerner. One of the girls is particularly interested in my iPad and her curiosity overcomes her shyness as she comes over to check it out. I appreciate the interaction.

The day is bright and cheerful and happy. I am entranced.

Chhiring comes back and we continue our hike. We slowly make our way uphill, not downhill, to reach the main trail between Lukla and Phakding.

Reading other accounts of hiking in this area, it's kind of hard to visualize what it's actually like. Even with pictures, you are only seeing a small segment of the trail. And that picture is only one "moment" along a trail that takes hours to traverse.

One word that comes to mind to describe the trail is "alive." There is an abundance of natural scenery, but there is also a plethora of small stores, homes, teahouses and lodges along the way. There is also a good bit of local traffic as the locals go about their business.

An hour or so into the hike, we encounter a yak train. I am very excited and pull out my camera to take pictures. This isn't just any yak train! This is my first yak train!

The very first yak train I encountered.

Chhiring gives instructions to "steer" far to the sides of the yaks, as they will walk right over you without a thought. It's not unknown for tourists to be trampled to death. It is also important to stay on the "cliff side" of the yaks. If you are on the "steep side" when they come through, it is a very real possibility you will be knocked into the abyss.

And we hike on. Prayer wheels are spun. Suspension bridges are crossed.

At one point, our timing is a bit off and we are stuck in the middle of a suspension bridge when a mule train comes along. Much better than a yak train, I think to myself.

We lean over the edge of the bridge as far as we can as the mules bounce and bump us with the large potato sacks they are carrying. The bridge bounces up and down. I am having fun.

Hanging out to take pictures as the mules pass by, Chhiring yells at me, "Run!"

Now a yak train is coming. This was not a good place to interact with these beasts and their huge horns. I run towards him and get off the bridge. Lucky for me, the yak driver had stopped the beasts from entering until I got off.

And we hike on. At the time, I didn't realize how far we were from Phakding. We hike for hours.

Everything looks so close on the map.

I vow along the way not to ask how much further to Phakding, but finally I cry uncle and ask.

"We are there already, ever since we crossed the last suspension bridge." He points up to the sign above me that indicates "Phakding Restaurant."

Oh! Here we are!

It has taken us three hours to get back "on schedule" to arrive at Phakding.

Chhiring takes off my backpack, I take off my daypack, and we stop for lunch. I sit outside on the sunny patio and Chhiring disappears inside. After a while, I am just plain curious where the heck he is. I go inside the restaurant, pull back a curtain and Chhiring is having lunch in the back.

Oh. Okay. I am curious what the situation is there, whether he is getting a free lunch or discounted lunch for taking me to this restaurant, which is great, or if this is coming out of his pocket from the fee he was charging. The same applied to his lodging in the evening. Did he have to pay for boarding or was this too subsidized for having brought business to the establishment?

For some reason, this remained quite a mystery to me for most of the trip, and Chhiring never brought it up. Perhaps he just viewed it as his personal business.

Maybe, on some level, he felt like he was getting "kickbacks," but I certainly didn't view it that way. I was very happy the lodges were taking care of the Sherpas that brought them business.

I had read that it is best not to offer to pay for your guide's meals. Some lodge owners might use this opportunity to charge for something that otherwise would be provided as a courtesy.

But on the flip side, if I was reading the situation incorrectly, Chhiring would be paying for many meals that I very happily would have paid for. Take care of those who take care of you. I didn't want him being stuck with this additional expense. What to do?

After lunch, we share the last of the homemade brownies I brought from Texas. It was that much less to carry!

It's now early afternoon and the trail follows along the beautiful and wild Dudh Kosi River. It's everything you would imagine a mountain river to be. The turquoise color is mesmerizing.

It's an intricate tapestry of rock and water. It's a powerful force of nature.

At times, we are right next to the river.

"Have you ever gone swimming here?" I ask.

Chhiring shudders and adamantly shakes his head no.

If someone didn't like you, they could push you in at certain points. I remember having this specific thought while on a rock slab that ran about five feet above the raging river below. It would probably take about five minutes to succumb to hypothermia in these frigid waters. It was kind of scary to think about.

On the way back along the Dudh Kosi near the end of the trip, there were three "aimless youths" meandering down the trail in the near vicinity to where I was hiking. Everyone else seemed to have an apparent purpose for their presence. They didn't seem to have one.

For some reason, this made me feel a bit uneasy, and I actually put a giant rock in my pocket for a bit of reassurance. Maybe it was that rushing river a few feet away that added to my unease. I am quite confident I was being overzealous.

That being said, it was quoted at one point during my journey by a teahouse attendant that "not all Sherpa are good."

Some recent documentaries of the Everest region have documented the changing attitudes among the younger Sherpa in the region, which I will not dwell on at length here. I will state that I hope they realize what a powerful legacy Tenzing Norgay has helped create and that many brave and dedicated Sherpas have carried on before them. I hope this legacy continues for generations to come.

We cross the Dudh Kosi on about six different suspension bridges. When I get to the lodge and check in for the evening, I still feel like I am swaying up and down on them.

We follow a number of ridges up and down along the river as we slowly make our way upstream for a number of miles.

During the easy stretches, I look forward to booking return tickets for myself and friends in the near future. During the uphill stretches, I start to have competing thoughts.

And one at a time, individual majestic peaks reveal themselves.

We continue on reasonably level terrain to Monjo. I was excited to hear we were approaching this town as it was a name I recognized. This is where I would get my TIMS card for $20 and then $30 a bit later down the road for my park permit. I would have walked past both stations without Chhiring's help. And they did check these things further down the road, one by a serious fellow in military garb.

I was checking out the scenery and a bit zoned out when I heard directly in front of me, "Slow down! Slow down! Slow down!" A uniformed attendant stood directly in front of me on the trail. I didn't realize this was a checkpoint. It's kind of an informal setting and blended in with the rest of the structures in the area. Chhiring ran interference and showed my credentials as I continued down the trail.

Chhiring had tried to convince me to stop at Monjo for the evening but I still had quite a lot of enthusiasm to get back on schedule. I tried to do the convincing.

"Don't you want to see your wife and lovely girl tonight?" They live in Namche. Chhiring was not taking on the role of cheerleader, nor of motivational speaker, at least when it came to getting to Namche that evening.

To make the point, he told one of his friends along the way what my plans were.

"You are going to Namche today?" His friend burst out laughing.

After Monjo, the trail changes. The trail changes to straight uphill.

Above us are two suspension bridges. The lower one is in disrepair. The higher one, which we will cross, is 100 meters or so above us. It seems impossibly far away. As I wrote in my journal, "It looked like an eternity."

After a bit more of trudging uphill, I begin to see the wisdom of Chhiring's suggestion of stopping for the evening. I am ready to call it quits.

"Okay, Chhiring. I'm ready to stop at the next lodge."

"There's no more lodges between here and Namche."

Oh, snap, as my son would say. We are committed.

"It starts getting steep in five minutes."

I began the routine of counting my steps. I would count up to 40, possibly up to 100 steps. By then, the oxygen supply to my body would be depleted. I would come to a stop, put my head on my pole and take 15 to 20 deep breaths.

"How much further?"

"About two and a half hours."

"That is not possible!" Why was he telling me this? This was no time to be joking around when I was at this stage of exhaustion. I just couldn't comprehend what his angle was. So I would be pleasantly surprised when we turned the corner and Namche was there?

"We are moving very slowly."

"No, we are moving very fast!" This I said with complete conviction and sincerity. (Well, at least until we got to the counting-breaths stage.)

Further up the trail, we encountered Michelle from Israel who had been hiking for eight days and was struggling up the hill as well.

She really lifted my spirits as misery loves company. We had quite a pleasant conversation, with her doing most of the talking. I was saving my breath. Eventually, my 20-breath rest routine was a bit slow for her and she carried on.

Without the peer pressure of keeping up with my new friend Michelle, I would occasionally stop to take 25 breaths.

Chhiring waited for me patiently.

One unique aspect of hiking in the mountains is you don't always have the option to stop. Well, at least not a very realistic option. When the parking lot with your car and access to the luxuries of civilization beckon just a couple of miles down the road, you aren't going to throw your backpack in the dirt and spend an unplanned night in the woods because you are a bit winded. You keep pushing.

If you are going on a day hike and your friends and family expect you back that same day, you keep pushing.

If your tent with food, shelter and warmth beckon a few hundred yards away, no matter what condition you are in, you keep pushing.

Swimming in the ocean, most people have enough sense not to swim out too far to sea. You may not get back. With mountaineering, it often seems that sense of proportionality is thrown to the wind. At least this seems to be the case from my personal experience.

Climbing a mountain can be a very symbolic act. "Climb every mountain" is a refrain that references the grandeur of the human spirit to overcome adversity. We just have to believe and set our minds to the task.

Contemplating the thought of summiting a grand peak, the mind on one level is not processing this as a mere physical act with rational thought. Instead, a dopamine cocktail rushes through the synapses of the frontal cortex, actualizing the concept that all things are possible. It is an epiphany realized with great joy and euphoria.

It's not until one is actually in the mountains that reality sets in and limits are reached. And then exceeded.

That was the case with my struggle to reach Namche Bazaar. I was utterly exhausted. If I was at the front desk of the lodge, I can't think of a solitary thing that would have urged me to take another single, solitary step, except those necessary to reach my actual room.

But at this point, I wasn't at the front desk of the lodge. Namche was nowhere in sight. And it was beginning to get dark.

I didn't want to sleep on the ground that evening, so I kept up my routine. Sixty steps. Twenty breaths. Fifty steps. Twenty breaths. Forty steps. Twenty breaths.

As darkness approached, so did Namche. We approached diagonally uphill from east to west. Spots of lights appeared here and there. By the time we reached the main streets of the town, it was completely dark. I continued my routine of rest stops. The horse was not sprinting to the finish line. There was still a bit of up to go.

Namche is a unique town built up along the side of a mountain that is amazingly symmetrical in shape. Climbing above the town and peering down, it looks like a gigantic bowl-shaped amphitheatre.

Near a row that looked promising to have my hotel on it, Chhiring said, "Give me my pack." We had swapped daypacks earlier and I was carrying his bag, as it weighed even less than my daypack.

"No. I can make it." I was willing to carry it the last 100 feet.

"But my wife is here. She will take it home for me."

I was in the middle of the walkway resting my head on my pole. I hadn't even seen her. I was too caught up in my own personal world of trying to suck in sufficient oxygen to make it the last 100 feet to the lodge.

So I got the opportunity to meet his wife Yangee, which I had actually been looking forward to. His precious little five-year-old girl Tenzing Doma was also present and started skipping along with us toward the lodge.

"Take my hand," she told me as we strolled the last fifty feet.

And this was one of the most memorable moments of my

trip. My depleted soul was replenished by this small spark of grace, this innocent gesture of kindness.

She took my hand and led me the last 50 feet to refuge.

We entered the lodge and the first thing I did was take photos of her and her dad before my imminent collapse. The tiny, little thing put on my daypack and started running around. It was almost as big as her. Just adorable.

They both came to my room and kept me company for a while, which I really appreciated, as I collapsed on the bed.

Chhiring and Tenzing Doma Sherpa in my room at the very nice Namche Hotel.

A few times in the past, after hiking past my limits in the mountains, I have reached a state where it hurts to take deep breaths. And this was one of those occasions. I was on the bed taking in short, shallow breaths. Those didn't hurt. Those I could handle.

And all the while my mind was reciting a mantra over and over again: Please don't leave. Please don't leave.

I needed Chhiring and Doma's human connection for just a little while longer.

--*-*-*-*-*-*

My room was a very nice room. Namche Hotel was and is a very nice hotel. In fact, the city of Namche Bazaar is a wonderful safe haven from the wilderness, offering an abundance of creature comforts.

Namche Hotel is pretty much like an ordinary hotel, except you have to hike a few days to get there. Another difference between this hotel and most hotels is that the rooms are not heated.

But the rooms are clean. They have bright lights. They have nice beds with warm blankets. They have regular bathrooms with flush toilets and sinks with clean water. They have good food at the lodge. Some rooms have in-room showers. Mine happened to be one.

After Chhiring and Doma left, I turned my energies to completing a few chores before crashing for the evening. It was going to take a great deal of mental and physical effort to even extricate myself from the bed, but I was motivated. I hadn't showered since Thursday evening in San Antonio and this was now Monday evening. Taking a shower was my main focus.

I knew there was a shower in my room, but would it be heated? I didn't allow my hopes to get too high, as it seemed too good to be true. I turned on the shower and felt the cold mountain water splash on my hands. I waited patiently. I continued waiting. Patience. Come on! Come on! Then, bingo, hot water miraculously arrived and flowed from the shower spigot!

It was glorious!
Then it was time to get out of the shower. And the room was near freezing. Ohhh, I had forgotten about that. In my fatigue, I had not prepared a towel or warm clothes to slip into. My body shivered uncontrollably as I raced out of the bathroom, a reasonably safe haven with trapped steam from the shower, into the even colder bedroom.

So this is the concept of cold I had heard about. Sometimes in South Texas, it is easy to forget what cold is. When I was packing for the trip, I even had passing thoughts of, oh, with all of these layers, do I really even need my down jacket?

I scurried to my backpack, opened it up and started pulling things out, madly tossing them onto the bed. I dug through the pack and pulled out -- everything. Strategically located at the very bottom were my wool underwear and towel. (I hadn't even noticed the hotel had provided a towel, located on the bed right next to my backpack.) It took over three minutes to get dressed.

I vowed to do better next time.

I then mustered up the energy to go eat dinner at the lodge.

The dining hall had an electric heater in the middle of it and was quite inviting. I ordered pizza and kept quietly to myself.

A few tables down, two couples were having a lively, upbeat discussion. They seemed friendly enough, but I was just too tired to engage in social interaction.

I didn't realize it at the time, but one of those couples was going to have a significant impact on my trip. But it wasn't going to happen that night.

I returned to my room and turned in for the evening. I woke up off and on during the night, contemplating the realities of the situation. This was only day two and I had already exceeded my limits. It is not a physical reality that I can keep this up.

Dark thoughts and doubts filled my psyche. I tossed around possibilities and maybes as the night continued to pass.

And then I came to a definitive conclusion before morning arrived. I can still see the thought bubble distinctly forming in all caps - typewritten.

I'm not going to make it. I just can't do this.

To be continued.

--*-*-*-*-*-*

Day 3 – Namche Bazaar

"I was a bit discouraged this morning." First journal entry for day three.

November 18, 2014.

I get out of my warm bed and start moving about in the cold room. No need to comb the hair. Just throw on a cap.

My room is in a wing of the hotel separate from the main lodge area. I step outside on my way to breakfast and have someone snap my picture with the mountains in the background. I distinctly remember the air being brisk and cold.

I climb the outside stairs up to the restaurant. I welcome the sight of the electric heater in the middle of the restaurant.

Namche Hotel is a very civilized place.

I order a coffee and chitchat with a group of Sherpa guides. In a bit, a couple came in.

It was the couple I had seen the previous evening but I was too tired to say hi. This morning, though, we greeted each other and they were kind enough to join me.

Dave and Bev presented themselves in a very positive and upbeat manner. They appeared to be just a bit younger than myself but definitely in an age group that I could relate to. They dressed well and were definitely not hippie-style backpackers. Dave was not even wearing a cap and had combed his hair.

Heading to breakfast at the Namche Hotel. It's cold outside!

I told them about my adventures for the last two days, including hiking into the night on day one – and day two. I told them what was really on my mind, that I was considering not going to EBC after all, that yesterday was an extremely hard day.

Replicating the experience from yesterday for the next nine days was not a physical possibility. Just the thought of a 400-meter day hike to Everest View Lodge later that day felt intimidating. Without hesitation, David made the pronouncement, "OH, YOU CAN'T DO THAT!"

He continued, "We just got back from there and it was great!"

I was shocked. They did not appear traumatized by a battlefield-type experience.

"You just got back from Everest Base Camp and you're still in good spirits?"

"Oh, definitely. It was fantastic!"

They explained that yesterday should be my hardest day and it was quite doable. I got out pad and pen and got to work taking notes.

Hike 20 minutes past Tengboche and stay at Deboche. They have a great lodge called Rivendell. The rooms have electric blankets and flush toilets.

I was in shock. I had no idea.

Then to Dingboche at the Good Luck Lodge. Very comfortable and with x number of amenities. You can even take a seven-minute outdoor hot shower and then run quickly to your room.

"Lol," I wrote in my journal. "I think one needs to see that to totally get the concept."

They didn't seem bothered by the fact they spent an extra night in Dingboche to acclimatize.

Lobuche, they admitted, was a bit sketchy but manageable.

From there they went straight up Kala Patthar above EBC and skipped spending the night at 17,000-foot high Gorak Shep.

This might be a good time to explain that Dave and Bev were using the term "EBC" and "Kala Patthar" synonymously. It is basically the same trek but with a better view.

Kala Patthar is 18,200 feet in height. The oxygen at this level is officially 50 percent of that at sea level. I consider it a remarkable achievement to reach this summit.

Many hikers to the region will choose Kala Patthar over EBC. The tradition is to climb Kala Patthar either in the morning or evening to watch the sunup or sunset. Sounds like a fun thing to do!

From Everest Base Camp proper, the summit of Mount Everest cannot be seen. It is blocked by the intimidating and monstrous Nuptse ridge. On the hike from Gorak Shep to base camp, though, the summit does come into view.

I felt my spirits renewed and physically I seemed to be recovering. Giving it a bit of thought, I had accomplished somewhere between 1.5 to two times the usual amount of hiking for day two. It made sense I would be physically, shall we say, "challenged."

Dave and Bev and I exchanged emails. I planned to keep them updated with the journal I was keeping. They left and I stayed in the dining area waiting for Chhiring.

After about five minutes, Bev came back and approached me again.

"Dave and I want you to have this for good luck." She then proceeded to hand me her headlamp.

I was floored. I had just met them an hour ago and they were offering this generous gift.

I was speechless for a few moments. "Thank you so much, but I can't accept this."

But Bev was insistent. I was touched and moved by this act of kindness.

I humbly accepted this gift and the spirit in which it was given. I would carry this headlamp with me, along with their good will.

I was actually in great spirits by the time Chhiring arrived. Things were turning around.

"Let's rock n roll!"

--*-*-*-*-*-*

Chhiring grabbed my daypack and we headed out. We stopped by a vendor just outside so I could buy some gloves. I was very happy with the $5 price that was quoted and there was no haggling back and forth. It was a much better value than the $39-$49 prices I was looking at stateside.

Back at the "intersection," where we had initially turned to go horizontally toward the lodge the night before, it dawned on me I had again forgotten my hiking pole -- this time in my room. It was way "too far" to go back to retrieve it. I would have to walk back 100 feet to the lodge, through the lodge, back outside, down a flight of stairs and down another hallway to where my room was. I wasn't about to backtrack.

Onward, Everest pilgrim!

Fortunately, there's a plethora of small outside vendors along the way and within moments I was the proud owner of a new ski pole, not even feeling the micro dent in my wallet.

Shopping is fun and easy in the Khumbu!

Chhiring seemed to be familiar with the proprietor, and it made me feel confident that Chhiring knew the lay of the land.

I was not at all adverse to having two hiking poles. I like the added stability they can give while hiking. A twisted ankle can end a trek in an instant.

I have also abused my knees in the past, the "piece de resistance" coming on a 90-mile hike on the Continental Divide. My ex-step-common-father-in-law (figure that one out) and myself were hiking in southern Colorado, starting about 80 miles east of the Silverton/Durango area, and we took just one too many wrong turns.

There was a perfectly defined trail that led up to the top of the Continental Divide about a day and a half outside of Silverton. We climbed the 1,200 feet or so to get to the top of the Divide and, bizarrely, the trail abruptly ended there. We needed to go down the other side to get back on route. We could eventually see the continued trail hundreds of feet down below running parallel with the Divide, but how were we going to get down there? We were determined to find a way down without backtracking. We followed what appeared to be game trails back and forth trying to find a way down, spending a lot of time and energy in the process.

Steep dropoffs kept blocking our way forward. Besides the cliffs, there were also steeply slanted areas, with no clear demarcation of the point of no return.

I made my way down at one point and realized that directly below me was a 12-foot-long, 45-degree slide of wet dirt. At the end of this slanted, slippery dirt was the abyss, falling away hundreds of feet. I could not make my way to the right or the left.

This was not good. I told Leroy to stay where he was, that I was coming back up. I turned around and realized I had to place my tennis shoe on one wet, slippery rock about two inches wide. I would have to place my wet, muddy tennis shoe on this, commit all of my weight and then stand up on it.

If I slipped, I couldn't see anything that would stop me from sliding off into the abyss.

After giving this a lot of thought, I yelled out to Leroy that I was going to hand up my backpack. That would make the "move" a lot less scary.

After carefully removing my backpack, I found it was just too heavy and awkward to hand it up to Leroy. I was afraid I would lose my balance. I then undid the straps attaching my sleeping bag and handed that up to Leroy, where he ferried this to a safe location before coming back for the rest of my backpack.

After this, I made my "move" on that wet piece of rock. For years afterwards, I would get heart palpitations just thinking about that moment.

I put my pack back together on safer terrain and we moved on. It was getting dark and there was a constant misty rain coming down. We finally found a gully with a stream running down it and climbed down this "path" in the dark, never quite sure when our way forward would be permanently barred or we would reach that point of no return.

After so much of this, we called it quits for the evening. There wasn't anything flat within miles, so we found a log to sit on in the steep gully. That was the best we could do.

Down below in the dark was the single light of another camper. We shone our light toward the camper, and he or she flashed back their light three times, prompting us to return the same signal if we were in distress. We gave a return signal of two flashes, which is the universal signal for just being miserable.

It continued to mist throughout the night. I tried to set up a tarp above us with various tree limbs in the area, but the water would just pool on the tarp and drip on us.

We never made it to sleep that night. In the morning, I climbed about 40 feet up the side of the gully in the thick mist. At the top of the gully, I could clearly view the wide, steep field of loose rock that extended hundreds of feet both above and below us. I could not see what was below the rockslide a few hundred feet down. The mist and angle of the decline kept this a mystery.

A decision had to be made. Commit ourselves further by going down or turn back around? We were scheduled to hike to the train track that ran between Silverton and Durango later that day. Families and friends were expecting us. It wasn't looking promising.

It was a tough decision, but we decided to turn around and climb back the way we had come. At this rate, it was possible we would come out of the mountains only one or two days late. If we messed up going downhill, it would exacerbate the situation even further.

We hiked up the rock field. Climbing from one rock to the next, I extended my knee a bit too far, put my weight on it and had one of those "uh-oh" moments.

Suddenly, after a week on the trail, I was concerned about weight. At the next rest stop, with my knee throbbing, I started digging through Leroy's backpack and was shocked at what I found.

"Why do you have an extra pair of jeans in here?"

He shrugged. "I dunno." He had never been backpacking before and I had not checked his pack before we left. I chastised him appropriately and convinced him to abandon some of his clothes on the spot.

At the top of the rock field, we found a small area that was flat enough to throw our sleeping bags and that's what we did.

The sun was peeking through on occasions but not often enough. The sun and clouds were mocking us, playing with our expectations. I crawled into my sleeping bag, face down, sleeping like the dead. I woke up about an hour later with drool on my sleeping bag. We then hiked back over the divide, back down, arriving where we had been about 30 hours previously. It was now dark and we were hiking through a marsh. I lost my balance and got my sleeping bag partially wet. That was not good either.

Leroy wasn't up for any more hiking through the dark, so we set up the tent and called it a night. It was cold and we had one wet sleeping bag. Amazingly, Leroy offered me the dry one and I wasn't too proud to take it. I kept the camp stove burning all night long to help keep Leroy warm.

The next morning, I checked out the topo map. If we hiked over 20 miles in a direction away from the railroad, we might make it to a small outpost of civilization, a certain dot on the map. And that's what we did. Before we made it out, though, my knees started locking up whenever we took rest stops.

At the small outpost of civilization, we were graciously offered a ride to the nearest pay phone 20 miles away. From there, we called our family, who called Randy and John, who were waiting for us in Durango. They had been doing campground camping and day hikes for the week.

Randy was pissed off (and that is the appropriate word) that I didn't offer to pay for the hotel room the night before, waiting for us to come out of the mountains a day late. Randy's father was a lawyer. He knew his rights. The fact that he had free-loaded an entirely free trip up to Colorado with us never entered his thought process. For months afterwards, he unsuccessfully hounded me for reimbursement.

On the long ride back home to Texas, we stopped to have breakfast and everybody sprinted into the restaurant, leaving me abandoned in the car. My knees were locked up and I couldn't get out of the cramped backseat.

And my knees haven't been the same since.

--*-*-*-*-*-*

After buying the ski pole, we turned north at this intersection, which meant we were going uphill. After a couple of blocks uphill, we turned 50 feet to the right and stopped at Chhiring's house to visit his wife Yangee and daughter Tenzing Doma.

We entered the two-story complex and climbed the steep wooden stairs. Their living quarters consisted of a single room. There was a bed with plenty of blankets, a sitting area and then a stove in the corner near the single window facing the street.

Yangee served us Sherpa tea, with plenty of refills. She got her daughter dressed for school, an arduous process with plenty of layers. I was surprised that she even had a tie on underneath her sweater.

Chhiring and I walked her up the steep hill toward the school. It was quite a climb for a five-year-old. I tried to walk quickly ahead of her to get a good photo of her and her father, but she kept running to catch up with me. When she met up with fellow students, she ran off without us the rest of the way.

My legs actually felt in reasonably good working order. Yesterday was more a test of my "system" as a whole.

As we continued to climb, I saw the very top of Ama Dablam off to the north, which I was very excited about.

View of the "Namche bowl." We arrived the day before from the lower left.

Many think of the Virgin Mary extending her arms in love and acceptance as they view the features of the mountain and its extending two ridges.

Along the path, Chhiring took a number of breaks to go off to the side and discuss "big business." I took advantage of this by relaxing on the soft brown grass on the hillside. I took off my shoes and socks and luxuriated on the feeling of the soft tundra grass underneath my feet. It was one of my favorite memories of the day.

As we climbed higher toward the top of the ridge, Ama Dablam came into full view. Wow!

Reaching the top of the ridge, our view was unhampered to the north. And there was the top of Mount Everest, rising

Taking a break above Namche heading to Everest View Lodge.

above the long knife-edged ridge of Nuptse, quite visible and prominent. What an incredible moment!

We reached Everest View Lodge, approaching from the south, walking through the grand structure. The north side of the lodge has large windows to take in the view of Mount

Everest. We proceeded outside to the elongated patio to get the full effect of the vista, with the crisp, fresh air adding to the ambiance of the moment.

To my surprise, far in the distance we could see Tengboche on the top of the ridge on the other side of the valley. The next day, we would loop to the east just far enough to swing around the side of the Namche bowl before heading due north toward Ama Dablan. We would then drop down to the river and then climb back up to the top of the opposite ridge

View from Everest View Lodge. Mount Everest is poking up above the Namche ridge on the far left of the photo.

to Tengboche, our destination for the next evening.

We actually planned to walk an extra 20 minutes past Tengboche to Deboche, but it's the same general area.

Chhiring's wife had offered to make lunch for us on our return, so we just had pricey soft drinks as the price of admission and made ourselves comfortable at one of the tables.

During the time we were there, Chhiring continued with multiple phone calls. He was very focused and intense. He was dealing with potential clients from India on a big guiding deal.

"One client is very easy to deal with. The other is very difficult."

When we left the restaurant, Chhiring looked at me with a guilty expression and told me, "I have to leave you to go to India. I am so sorry, but this is big money deal."

"No, you can't do that!" It just came out. It was my honest reaction to the news. Chhiring was the perfect guide. I didn't want to lose him.

He repeatedly apologized and I accepted and wished him well. I wanted him to do what is best for his family. I completely understood. Kind of.

He told me it was his duty to find me a good guide (or did he just say porter?) to take me the rest of the way.

"Will he speak English?"

A brief pause. "Yes, I will find you guide who speaks good English."

He was a bit quiet on the way down the hill. He still had a lot on his mind.

"I hope this deal works out," he told me. He planned to go to Lukla that evening before flying off to India. I was impressed. He must really be a good guide!

We reached his home and climbed the scary steep wood ladder to the top floor. His wife made me a pancake with a spicy cheese sauce served on the side. Very interesting flavor.

As mentioned previously, Chhiring informed me the going

Chhiring and Yangee Sherpa.

rate was $20 per day for a porter, $25 per day for a porter/guide. I have heard of situations where hikers have paid for both a porter and also a guide, practically doubling the expense. I chose the porter/guide option.

Since this was the last time I would probably see Chhiring, I wanted to settle accounts with him. Should I pay him up front for twelve days, $300, or pay the next guide his proportionate share? Chhiring requested the $300 up front and I trusted him enough to do this. I also gave him a nominal tip on top of this. It was still vivid in my mind his efforts to find me on day one and his assistance since then.

Chhiring looked confused when I handed him the tip. "This is for me?" I assured him it was and again thanked him for all of his help.

I started climbing down the hill to my lodge and I saw Michelle sitting at a table in a small courtyard to my left. I detoured over to join her, along with a young hiker named James. James seemed like a pretty sturdy fellow. One of his main topics of conversation was getting pain medication for his knees.

I got the impression he was a bit sweet with Michelle. James asked if I wanted to join them to go to some museum in the area, but I declined. I had other business to attend to. But I did appreciate the offer.

Continuing on to Namche Hotel, I stopped at a couple of stores to look for a charger for my iPad. The iPad's battery was completely drained, despite being plugged into American-style outlets in my room and at the front counter of the lodge's registration area/restaurant. I was using the iPad to keep my journal updated and this was at risk.

The plugs in my room had an off/on switch next to the plug that would not allow the iPad adapter to fit properly. It worked fine for my other electronics. In the restaurant, the power strip seemed to be loosy goosy and I could not tell if it was charging. It wasn't. All of these issues, though, made it difficult to come to a conclusion whether my adapter truly was broken and needed replacement.

The lady at the front desk offered three adapters to try in my room, all to no avail.

Okay. Time to go to the Internet cafe. Or Internet room. It was a small electronics office with a couple of computers available for surfing. It was right outside the lodge and a part of the lodge structure. I took my iPad with me and gave it to the owner there and asked if he by any chance had any kind of connections to get it charged.

After playing around with it, he figured out I had a bad cable. He switched it out and it started charging.

"Can I buy that from you?"

"Oh, no. This is my only one."

"Let me guess. It's the only one in Namche?" He shrugged his shoulders. "Maybe not."

I had actually encountered this problem before, so I asked if it was a bad cable or bad adapter at the end of the cable. After he played around with it a bit, he diagnosed it as a bad cable.

"Oh, I can sell you the cable. It's the adapter I only have one of."

I was ecstatic. My iPad was my contact with the outside world.

I surfed the Internet a bit while he confirmed it was continuing to charge. After a while, I started shivering from the cold in the small Internet room and said I would try to continue charging it in my room. He charged me $3.50 for the cable and Internet use.

I bought a slice of apple pie from one of the world's highest bakeries and took it back to the room. Yum!

At about 6:00 that evening, Chhiring's cousin's brother came by to introduce himself. (Wouldn't that make him his cousin also?) He was going to be my new guide.

"My name is Kaji Sherpa."

"Kaji?"

"Kaji Sherpa."

I took a "nap" then until about 11:00 that evening and then decided it might be a good idea to take a shower. I wasn't sure if there was going to be hot water at 11:00 at night. Sometimes there is a time period involved.

At registration, I distinctly remembered them saying, "Your hot shower is ready." Energy and resources can be saved by not having the hot water heater on constantly.

I ran the water for quite a while and it was still ice cold. There was no way I was taking a cold shower. I checked one more time and it was lukewarm.

Then hot. Booya!

This time I prepared appropriately and had a towel and warm clothes waiting. When I got out, I was moving fast enough to hear my heart beating rapidly. I would guesstimate I cut my previous time in half.

I had survived running into the frigid room after a hot shower! Not exactly mountain man material, but I was making progress.

To be continued.

--*-*-*-*-*-*

Day 4 – Namche Bazaar to Tengboche/Deboche

November 19, 2014.

I was hoping for not a lot of drama today and I got my wish. Everything went quite smoothly, thank goodness.

Except for one major possible snafu I learned about this evening.

The rustling next door woke me up shortly after 5:00, so by 5:30 I got up and started packing. I am getting a bit more organized and was ready for coffee by 6:30. Kaji and I had agreed to meet at 8:00.

I was hoping Kaji would get there a bit early.

Maya, the proprietor of the lodge, agreed I could leave some things to pick up on my return on approximately November 25. I had already separated out the things earlier that morning. I gave them a large plastic bag with a kilo or two of clothes and food items I thought I could live without, like the heavy glass jar of almond butter. (It's delicious. You should really try it!)

After having tied a big knot at the top of the plastic bag, they took it to their back room for safekeeping.

Maya also was kind enough to call the Rivendell Lodge in Deboche to make a reservation for that evening. I truly appreciated that.

Kaji showed up on time. Good start. He is a quiet, helpful young man, 20 years old. His English is somewhat limited so it will probably not be as interactive and personal as before, but I am quite confident everything will go well.

We went by his porter lodge to pick up his bag. Probably not even a kilo in weight. I am impressed.

Early on, while still climbing up through the town of Namche, we passed a group of trekkers. One of the girls had a huge, flat-panel shiny thing hanging off of her that covered half of her back.

"Are you transmitting live to the Internet?"

"No, it's a solar panel for my electronics."

It's a brave new world out there, folks.

Up ahead, another large group had gathered around a doorway with multiple cameras clicking away. I had a feeling I knew what was going on. Yep. A cute Nepali little girl was grinning and smiling away for her paparazzi. Everyone was having a good time.

The route today was fairly level for the first three hours, with reasonable ups and downs. Not sure what the distance is. One of my favorite sights for the day was looking at the reasonably flat trail ahead as we swerved around the sides of the mountain.

We were joined by another porter who kept Kaji company much of the first three hours. He was carrying two backpacks strapped together. I asked him how much it weighed and he told me 30 kilos. Which makes sense. I have seen a number of tour companies state that each trekker

Mount Everest pokes up above the Namche ridge. The trail is flat heading north before dropping down to the right to the river valley and climbing back up to Tengboche.

Kaji Sherpa with wonderfully flat trail in the background.

is allowed 15 kilos to be carried by a porter. I told him it looked like 40. He smiled and gave me a thumbs up.

For most of the morning, a yak train was chasing us and it was a challenge to keep ahead of it, especially with all of the photographic opportunities that were available. You could hear the "ox bells" ringing and the yak drivers singing to their herd.

The Internet warned about dust issues on the trail and this is the first day I noticed it. Both yaks and trekkers would kick up the dust. There were lots of yaks. It would settle down fairly quickly, but it was enough that the trekkers wearing balaclavas/buffs seemed like the smart kids on the block.

We dropped down to the bottom of the valley, where the bridge crosses the Dudh Kosi, at the three-hour mark. Kaji and his friend spontaneously took off their packs. Evidently, this is a designated rest stop. Next to the Dudh Kosi is always a beautiful spot to rest. I offered to buy them a soft drink.

I handed the lady 1,000 rupees ($10) and she just seemed really pissed off about it. Not sure what the problem was. A water and two sodas wound up costing 800 rupees, a bit over $8 at the exchange rate I could get in Namche.

The "yak tax" was kicking in more and more as we got further down the trail.

After our break, the test piece lay ahead. It was now time to cross the bridge and ascend 550 meters to Tengboche.

"How long do you think it will take?"

"Two hours," says Kaji's friend.

"I think maybe three."

Check point after crossing the Dudh Kosi, getting ready to climb back up to Tengboche.

Before crossing the bridge, I finally remember to pull out my new altimeter and start playing with it.

We started crossing the bridge and it seemed more bouncy than usual. I looked behind me to see a porter bearing down on me with his large load.

We started at about 3,350 meters at the river. Chhiring had told me the climb to Tengboche was 500-550 meters. I was interested to see how accurate he was. It was 550 meters.

Soon after the bridge there was a checkpoint manned by an

official in military garb. I noticed this checkpoint so I didn't get yelled at. Right before I left Chhiring's home yesterday, I had remembered to ask for my permits back. If I had forgotten them, this could have been quite awkward.

The climb was challenging but not overwhelming, like I experienced on the climb to Namche. In fact, it is possible this climb and the Namche climb are similar - the only difference being the extra hours of trekking I had put in prior to climbing up to Namche.

Well, actually, I also had a couple of extra days to acclimatize by this point. I am sure this helped immensely.

In other words, I was coming to an understanding that this hike doesn't have to be "as" arduous as I had made it. Just hike the allotted amounts each day and allow extra days for unforeseen circumstances.

The altimeter was a good motivational tool as I checked our progress up the hill. It made the climb more finite rather than an unending slog.

By an hour we had climbed 300 meters. By two hours we had reached Tengboche at the top of the hill.

I can honestly say the climb was made more enjoyable by thinking of my friends that were staying in touch via the Internet. They were great cheerleaders. A bit tired and winded? I was encouraged to have the "eye of the tiger"!

Another ridge to climb? Well, that's just great! Is that the best you've got?

My friend Jerry suggested I go into "beast mode." That never quite happened. I would have needed a yak for that.

Viewing north from the Tengboche square is the path toward Dingboche and Everest. To the west of the square is Tengboche Temple.

The entry into Tengboche was sudden. You reach the top of the ridge, turn a corner and there it is. By spinning in a circle, you can see the whole thing. A bakery and small shopping area was straight ahead north, the monastery to our left, and a lodge or two to the right. Oh. And a spectacular view of Mount Everest and Ama Dablam also sprang into view just as we topped the ridge.

After a short break, we started downhill to Deboche. (Not to be confused with Dingboche, our next day's destination.) A lone female hiker was coming up the ridge and asked in a soft European voice, "How much further?" I looked at my handy altimeter and informed her just another 50 meters. That seemed to bring her some comfort.

In less than 20 minutes we were in Deboche. We had completed the day's hiking by 1:30. I was ecstatic! No night hiking today!

We go to check in and I don't even ask about price. I am sure it is more than the $12 I paid for food and lodging my first evening, but I am confident it will be reasonable.

The proprietor Jangmo walks me toward my room. Directly in front of it was a hallway that had long benches along the wall. I thought to myself, hey, if the inn is overflowing you could have people sleeping there.

She opened the door and it was a plain room with two beds. Oh, no private bathroom. Okay.

"Can you tell me where the showers are located?"

"They are right there." The door had swung open and

covered the entrance to the bathroom, complete with flush toilet and shower. (This trek is becoming more and more mainstream, much to the chagrin of Sir Edmund Hillary and many other purists.)

I asked if there was a time schedule for taking a hot shower. I did my research. From here on out, the hot water is from solar power, so resources are limited and showers are only available at certain times.

"Oh, no. You can take it now or in the morning. Not a problem."

I tested the water and it was scalding hot.

Kaji was just kind of hanging around and I wasn't sure why.

"Kaji, where are you sleeping tonight?"

"Oh, right there." He pointed to the benches.

I was a bit taken aback.

"Right there?"

"Yes. It's okay for Nepali people."

It just felt weird for him to be right there in front of my room. In all honesty, I have no idea where Chhiring slept on our first night out.

Kaji and I went to the lodge dining area and got a seat by the window with a great view of Mount Everest.

He asked what I wanted to eat and showed me a menu. In the back of my mind I was thinking, why are you being my waiter? I ordered vegetable fried rice. He pulled out a ledger, wrote my name down and what I ordered, just like Chhiring did on day one. I assumed that somehow this affected their ability to get subsidized/free lodging and food. Kaji also got the same dish.

A few hours later he asked what I wanted for dinner. I told him I couldn't even think about that right now.

"For 6:00 o'clock."

"Okay." I placed my order, still wondering how the system works. If I didn't order dinner, would he then have to pay for his?

The norm is to hang out in the restaurant until you are ready to go to bed. It's much colder in the rooms. (It's 31.6 degrees in my room as I write this in my sleeping bag and down coat on.)

At 3:30, they crank up the wood fire stove in the very center of the dining room.

It's an interesting setup. There are benches directly in front of the stove on three sides where the porters hang out. Along the windows are conventional tables where the trekkers sit and eat.

At first, I was a bit disturbed by the seating arrangements by "class." But as the night wore on, things seemed to work out okay. The Sherpas sat around the stove, were toasty warm and enjoyed chatting among themselves. There were no hard and fast rules. The guides would come out to chat with clients and the trekkers would barge in closer to the stove to get warmed up.

While working on my journal, Ilsa from Johannesburg asked if she could sit down. A large trekking group had come in and seating was limited.
Ilsa was high tech and had both her iPad and iPhone working steadily, staying in touch with friends and family. Every few minutes, her chat app would pop up with a new message.

The communal center of the lodges is the wood/yak dung-burning stove. It's a good thing.

It may have been 30 minutes before we spoke.

She was a psychologist who had focused in family

counseling and had just sold her successful practice.

She was on day 13 of her three-week trek with three other friends. The guiding agency seemed to be taking good care of them. They brought along yaks to haul supplies and had their own personal chef to prepare meals.

She had just returned from Lobuche that morning after suffering a sudden attack of altitude sickness.

Lobuche is the launching point for the hike to Gorak Shep, Everest Base Camp and Kala Patthar.

At about 3:00 that morning, she started suffering from an extreme headache. She said she could feel her brain expanding. Up to that point, she was doing great and had no warning symptoms at all.

A few hours later, her guide told her she needed to go back and that's what she did. She said Deboche was her new "base camp" until the rest of her friends returned. She seemed happy with that prospect as she watched the sunset play out on Mount Everest.

Ilsa also informed me that the airport at Lukla would be closed on November 23 and 25 for some type of government "summit." My scheduled flight to Lukla was November 25, with my international flight leaving the next day. This was disconcerting news.

"So they are having a summit in Lukla?"

"No. I think in Kathmandu."

"So why are they closing the airport in Lukla?"

"I think they are closing down all of the airports in Nepal. It's a security issue."

"How does having flights from Lukla to Kathmandu pose a security threat?"

"Well, I don't know."
The whole situation made absolutely no sense to me and I tried to wrap my mind around this new concept. The rules in Nepal are definitely different.

--*-*-*-*-*-*

As dinner approached, I eyed the large group again and asked Ilsa, "How is the water heated here?"

"By solar power."

"That's what I thought. I better go and get a shower while I can."

I asked Jangmo to rent a towel, as I didn't want to get mine wet before it was necessary.

"Oh, there is not a towel in your room? And it is probably best to wait to morning to take a hot shower. All the hot water is gone now from large group."

I felt older and wiser. I should have jumped in the shower right away in the early afternoon and beat the rush. Hot water is a limited resource at this stage of the trek.

I go back to my room to get ready for bed and I immediately start trembling from the cold. My hands are shaking so much it is difficult to put on my two layers of wool before adding my down jacket.

I put the sleeping bag under the blankets and crawl in for the night with my down jacket still on.

I sleep until about 12:30 and get up to use the bathroom and check the water temperature. My thinking was, if there is no hot water now, there certainly won't be any in the morning.

I let it run for a while to see if it will "finally" turn warm. It doesn't. After a minute or two, Jangmo knocks on my door.

"Are you okay in there?"

Evidently, she heard the water running in the middle of the night and wanted to know what the heck was going on. Why was this crazy Westerner wasting precious resources in the middle of the night?

I quickly turned off the frigid stream of water, a bit embarrassed. "Yes, everything's fine."

I made peace with the fact I wasn't getting a hot shower in Deboche. I had missed my window of opportunity. The solar panels weren't going to kick in by the time we left in the morning. No worries. I was just at that point of the hike.

Last journal entry for the day: It seems my iPad is too cold to recharge well. Future reports may be spotty.

--*-*-*-*-*-*

Day 5 – Deboche to Dingboche

First journal entry for the day: "Very pleasant accommodations at Deboche, although it got down to 31 degrees in the room last night."

November 20, 2014.

I wake up to the frosty room and check the shower to see if there was any hot water and to my surprise it was now steaming hot.

Evidently, I was misinformed about the water being solar heated.

I held out hope that the information about the Lukla airport closing was also a bit of misinformation.

It was the beginning of day five of my journey and I was still taking hot showers! The route to Everest Base Camp continues to become more and more gentrified.

Kaji and I had breakfast and then I went to settle my tab.

The Rivendell Lodge is not your garden-variety $2 lodge. It was approximately $25 per night. With food, Internet service and drinks, the bill totaled around $45.

We were ready to leave by 8:15 and it was quite cold. The gloves came on for the first time and the wind shell was added for extra warmth. We headed north straight toward Mount Everest, which graced the skyline during much of our morning walk. We walked for about 45 minutes gradually downhill along the wooded path before crossing the river

Leaving Rivendell Lodge in Deboche.

Heading north toward Ama Dablam. Dingboche is located on the western side of this magnificent peak.

and heading back up a steep incline.

The day as a whole seemed to be marked by a lot of ups and downs without gaining much altitude. That was going to be saved for the end of the day.

When we reached Pangboche in about an hour and a half, Kaji went shopping for a pair of sunglasses and I was checking out the down overgloves. I asked how much his sunglasses would be. If they were $150, I wasn't going to get them. They were $4. Between the gloves and glasses, I got change back from 2,000 rupees.

At the time, I didn't realize we were in the town of Pangboche. I didn't even realize we were in a town. Thinking back on it, though, it's more of a town than Deboche.

Deboche, in my mind, is not a town. There was the Rivendell Lodge, the first structure I remember encountering, and then another lodge about 50 yards further down. Even further down the trail, there were a few more structures here and there, but no centrally developed area. A number of lodges were also in mid-construction in the area. The future is coming.

Pangboche has a bit more to it, more structures on the side of the trail in a somewhat limited area. They don't have signs announcing you have crossed the city limits, though.

We continued on, stopping at a small village for lunch at a small restaurant that Kaji gestured toward. We sat outside in an open area next to a small brook. Duncan and Gin were eating at the next table out in the front yard. I had tomato soup and Gin had spaghetti with tomato sauce.

"I think they used the same sauce for both," Gin surmised. Nearby, a couple of baby yaks were drinking from the small stream and a toddler was emulating washing clothes in the cold water.

Baby yaks and this toddler washing clothes in the stream kept us entertained at our lunch stop.

As Gin snapped pics of the baby yaks, she announced, "Oh, they are sooo cute!"

"Yeah, but then they grow up." That got a laugh.

The landscape changed as we climbed into a zone of tundra grass and shrub. We climbed through beautiful, desolate valleys with wild, beautiful rivers flowing below.

We got a late start after lunch, so I didn't think we would make it in the five hours that Kaji had estimated it would take. We only had 300 meters to go for the day and I was confident it was going to be another easy day.

You can't get much more isolated than this residence, located in this harsh, cold and demanding environment. These children offered me handfuls of grain that they were snacking on.

But the trail kept going up and down through the valleys and I could tell the last 300 meters would be saved for the very end.

I take a rest by leaning on my poles and I hear crunch. In my upper soft-shell pocket, I had cracked my reading glasses in half. Oh, crap.

We drop down into a valley to cross a small bridge late in the afternoon and lose most of the altitude we had gained throughout the day. From here, we would climb the final 300 meters. And I was beginning to fade. I tried a variety of motivational speeches and mantras to keep myself going.

Most of the elevation for the day was lost climbing down to this bridge. Time to climb north again to Dingboche!

"My family is with me. My friends are with me."

It helped to a degree. But as the day wore on and my exhaustion grew, I accepted the fact that this was just going to be a grind, pure and simple. There was no energy left for an internal pep talk. It just needed to be done.

Somewhere behind us, the trail had branched off from the trail going to Pheriche. Pheriche is an alternate stopping point to Dingboche. The trails to Pheriche and Dingboche would again join together at Dughla further down the trail.

Our trail went up steadily from here, constantly climbing straight to the north, higher and higher above the desolate, wild valley below. We were now way above the tree line.

The trail had a bit of scary exposure. It was a good thing to pay attention. It was plenty safe unless you zoned out, forgetting where you were and what you were doing, which I am capable of doing at times.

The couple from the restaurant was having difficulty too. By this point, there was just general exhaustion and fatigue. The usual. We were getting higher and the air was getting thinner.

There were moments on the trail of exaltation and some of complete exhaustion. One moment I was thinking what a shame my friends couldn't make it. The next, I was thanking God I wasn't exposing them to this experience of extreme fatigue.

We eventually saw the town of Dingboche below us and it was quite a relief.

That must have kicked off some adrenaline with the couple and their pace quickened.

"You know, there is no shame in taking a break occasionally," I called out to them. They kept walking and left me behind by about 50 yards.

Why am I not keeping up with them? I just couldn't figure it out. Then it came to me: They were a couple of decades younger than me.

Oh, crap. How did that happen?

*_*_*_*_*_*_*_*

Looking north toward Dingboche. The next day we would have an acclimatization climb to the western ridge, then reclimb this again the following day on our way to Dughla.

They stayed at the first lodge we ran across.

"Do you want to stay with them?" Kaji asked.

"No. They left me behind."

We had reached Dingboche in five hours and 15 minutes. Of course, time has its own special dimension in the mountains. It felt like much longer.

Within ten more minutes we reached the lodge recommended to me previously, but we couldn't figure out how to reach it. Kaji asked some locals and they indicate just up the way.

We climb over a stone wall that was partially knocked down to half height to make access easier, cross on the side of a field and jump another stone wall.

I knocked off one of the stones in the process and felt bad. I am sure someone was very proud of their fence. They had put a lot of work into it.

We reached Hotel Good Luck and it was no Rivendell. My expectations had been set too high. I needed to adjust them.

"We only have common room available."

"You mean I have to sleep with other people?"

We weren't able to communicate effectively so I asked to see the room.

It was a room with a single bed and four walls.

"How much?"

"Two dollars."

I sighed. I was too tired to go jumping over stone fences all over town looking for available space so I agreed.

Along the hallway, the unoccupied rooms were open and I noticed some had two beds instead of one.

I hauled my backpack over to the room with two beds so I could continue with my time-tested system of organizing my things by taking everything out of my backpack (well, not quite everything) and throwing it on the opposite bed for easy access.

When I was situated, I went back to the restaurant/ registration area and Kaji was having his hot tea. No one was around to bring me any, so I waited around for the attendant to return.

Next to Kaji and myself was a loud, rowdy group of porters playing cards. They were speaking loudly and gesturing dramatically, rough in manner and appearance. At first I thought they were trekkers from a nearby country. I was surprised when they started speaking Nepali to Kaji.

Their mannerisms reminded me of a bunch of gremlins. Evidently, someone got a mogwai wet.

They seemed to even make Kaji nervous. I assumed they were from a different ethnic group than Kaji and I just couldn't see them playing well together.

Was he going to have to bunk down with these guys? I felt bad. They just emanated bad biorhythms.

When the lodge operator finally returned, just for curiosity I asked how much the two-bed room was. I showed him the key that I found and had taken from the room.

He immediately turned to Kaji and started yelling. Or at least talking excitedly. "Speaking with conviction" would be one way to phrase it. The harangue continued for quite a while. My own fatigue was perhaps altering my perception of the events, but I was not happy with the way Kaji was being addressed.

No further information was relayed to me. Everything that needed to be said had been conveyed to Kaji.

Evidently, a big group was coming in tomorrow and I would have to move. Kaji informed me of this once everything settled down.

I went to take a rest and noticed I was more tired than I thought. I laid my cloth liner directly on the bed, put my sleeping bag on top of that, then put the blanket over everything.

I couldn't sleep and I couldn't get warm. I felt my body was shutting down and not producing enough heat.

While lying there, I started ruminating on the whole situation at the lodge and started to become upset. My mind got caught in a loop that spiraled into even further agitation.

How dare they yell at Kaji! Yell at me, but don't yell at my Sherpa!

My psyche was cooking up a witch's brew, a toxic cocktail of negativity. Adding to my general unhappiness was the image of Kaji interacting with the porters from hell.

I came to the only logical conclusion that my state of mind allowed. The present situation was intolerable.

Am I really that pissed off? Yes, I am. Let's get the hell out of here. I don't care if it causes a scene. We are leaving.

I start going through a mental checklist of all the different steps it would take to move to a different lodge.

I will have to get out of bed. I will have to repack my backpack. Ugh. I need to track down Kaji. I need to "check out." We would then need to go hopping over stone walls, hiking through fields looking for other lodging. It seemed overwhelming, but it had to be done.

First things first, I calmly and practically tell myself. I need to extricate myself from this sleeping bag and get out of bed. This needs to be done. Deep breath. Gather your strength.

My inner Buddha attempts to give guidance and wisdom: A journey of a few hundred yards begins with the first step.

I sit up in bed, still inside my sleeping bag. I stay in this position for a few moments. And then a few moments longer. Forward movement ceases. I am empty and depleted.

I then collapse back into bed. Deep sigh. I just don't have the strength to move.

I was stuck in the Hotel California. I could check out any time I want, but I could never leave.

--*-*-*-*-*-*

Time passes. I get up and go to the main lodge. The fire is going and I park next to it. I finally begin to warm up.

"Do you know what they are burning in here?" I ask the cute trekkers from Singapore that are also hovering near the fireplace.

"Firewood."

"Good!" was my reply.

They had no idea what I was talking about. I had read that yak dung is what kept the lodges warm in the Khumbu region.

I looked out the window and didn't see a tree anywhere in sight. I don't think there was one within miles.

Firewood? You can't believe everything you hear.

In conversation by the stove, I casually mention to the two young Singaporeans that I was curious whether they were going to up my rate of $2 a night since I now had two beds.

They looked baffled.

"Excuse me?"

I then remembered some of these folks were on package tours that paid quite a bit more money than I was spending doing this solo. I made it a point not to bring up this subject, as there was just no need.

"Oh, never mind," was my reply.

Earlier in the trip I had been point blank asked how much I was paying for my guide.

"Do you really want to know?" I paused for the response.

When I told them I had paid $300, they were visibly disturbed. They had paid $6,100 per person for their tour, not including airfare. Bringing up this subject was a quick way to shut down a conversation.

I was still feeling whipped and didn't think I was capable of social interaction, but the folks sitting at the next table along the long bench soon were kind enough to include me in their conversations. They confirmed they too had heard about the airport shutting down and were scheduled to leave the same day as me, November 27. We were just going to have to wait and see what happened.

I asked them to excuse me and I actually laid down and crashed for a bit along the padded bench we were sitting on next to the wall. It was super comfortable -- and warm. I wanted to spend the night there rather than return to my freezing room.

Kaji reminded me, "Be sure to wear something over your head tonight. You need to stay warm."

I waited reasonably late to return to the room. It was going from the light and warmth of the lodge to the dark and cold. I put on two layers of wool, my soft-shell and then my down jacket before crawling into the sleeping bag and pulling the two blankets over the top.

I lay in bed thinking, only two more hiking days to Everest Base Camp. I'm getting closer!

--*-*-*-*-*-*

Day 6 – Dingboche

November 21, 2014.

Throughout the night I wake up to take one layer off at a time until I am down to my woolies. The covers had slid off the bed and I was still warm. The temperature again went down to 31 degrees. It felt like it was in the twenties.

I had multiple dreams that just didn't make sense, even while I was dreaming them. I am confident it was caused by the altitude and exertion.

On previous occasions when I camped at high altitude, I had dreams that would continue even after I was awake and sitting up in my sleeping bag. I would try to stop the narrative of the dream, fight against it, but it was as if the dream was stronger than my own reality. It could be quite disturbing.

While on Mount Rainier, I woke up my climbing partner David in the middle of the night and asked him to talk to me. I needed something to latch onto. I was trying to figure out which was the true reality. Try explaining that concept to someone at 1:30 in the morning.

As soon as I got up, I started packing. Kaji told me his brother worked at another lodge and I was happy to move there.

When he said "brother," I was coming to understand he meant someone from his own ethnic group.

We started hiking uphill and stayed at one of the higher

lodges in the village, Valley View Lodge. I only had to stop twice to catch my breath on the way over. The air is beginning to get thin.

Happily relocated at the Valley View Inn in Dingboche.

I wasn't concerned about price, but I asked the owner what the cost was.

"$2.00." (He actually said 200 rupees but I am just simplifying things.)

And that's for two beds.

That is a phenomenal price, but I wound up doing the Cadillac version of the plan.

Three meals, about $15.

Tea service, maybe $2.
Unlimited Internet, $10.
Charging my electronics for two hours, $6.
Couple liters of water, $6.
Other item discussed later, $4.

So we are looking at $45 or so. And in the process, they take good care of my porter-guide. No complaints here.

I immediately liked the lodge more than our previous accommodations. It was much more airy, open and cleaner. I liked my room a lot more too.

Before I had been told there were rooms where you just had to share the toilet with one other room. I wondered how that worked. Would you have to latch the other door when you went to the restroom? What if you forgot to unlatch it?

As I faced the small entrance, my room was to the left, another room was to the right, and in the hallway in between was a toilet with its own entrance. Now I understood. You would actually leave your room and immediately go back into the toilet.

Internet was available for $10 a day and recharging your electronics was $3 an hour.

I was very happy to be here!

Kaji pretty much insisted we do a day hike, but he would take it easy on me. He said 100 yards but I figured that was just to get me out of the house. I was right.

I am very glad we went on the hike. We went up the ridge

to the west of the lodge. When we crested it, I admired my first view of Lobuche Peak.

On the other side of Dingboche, across the valley, was a great side view of Ama Dablam.

At the top of the ridge to the west of Dingboche, leading to Dughla, Lobuche and beyond. The western arm of Ama Dablam is in the background. Dingboche lies below.

Kaji showed me the direction toward Lobuche, where we were heading the next day. We would just continue from this point to the northwest.

"How high is Lobuche again?"

"Five thousand meters."

I attempted to digest the number. My altimeter was reading 4,250 at the lodge.

"Are there ups and downs?"

"Yes. Ups and downs to Dughla, then up."

"What's the angle of climbing? Like this or like this?" I gestured two degrees of angle with my hand.

He indicated the steeper one.

"But some of the hiking is flat."

Still, I attempted to gear up to the fact that tomorrow was going to be a tough day.

It wound up being a great 220-meter hike with great views. I was glad I did it. There was still plenty more hill to climb but I was satiated.

Back at the lodge, I noticed the sign on the lodge wall indicating "gas shower available."

I asked the lodge owner how much a shower was. He told me $4.

I considered for a moment whether it was worth it.

Just joking.

My learning curve had reached a point that I knew afternoons were the best time to shower. Much warmer!

The lodge owner showed me to the shower, which was definitely clean enough. And it had a great view of the surrounding peaks through the window. He pointed to the red lever, which was angled parallel to the ground.
"Here is off. Up is hot."

Simple enough.

I start the shower and it is scalding hot. It could damage you. I basically stood outside of the flow of water, wetted my washcloth and then wetted it again when I was ready to rinse off. I wetted the washcloth as low as possible to give the water a chance to cool on the way down, to no avail. I wound up scalding the back of my hand, which took weeks to heal.

When I was basically through with my shower, I was messing with the knob and it went below "off" (parallel to the ground) and went even lower. And the water temperature became perfectly warm, not scalding.

Oh, geez. I had been in there long enough, but I thought I owed myself at least a minute of luxuriating.

I didn't suffer when I turned off the water because the super-heated steam had warmed up the shower room.

Overall, I give a thumbs up to this shower. This was going to be my last shower until returning to Namche Bazaar.

By 3:30, it was already shivering cold and I go to hang out at the lodge.

They haven't lit the stove yet so it is cold in there too, but I take a seat in the sun.

By 4:30, one of the Sherpas points to the stove, then the registration desk, then to the door while speaking to his fellow porter.
I knew what he was saying in Nepali. "Get the owner to light the darned stove."
He then turns to me and says, "I'm cold!"

"Me too!"

I have a brilliant epiphany at this moment. I order hot tea.

By 5:00, the owner comes in and pours a clear liquid into the stove and lights it.

"Kerosene?"

"Yes."

By 5:30, he returns with a load of yak dung and starts tossing it into the stove. He adds more kerosene to the mix.

Ding, ding, ding, ladies from Singapore! That wasn't wood they were burning last night!

By 6:00, I am fending for a place in front of the stove to quickly warm up after returning from my room.

Kaji is smiling and chatting with his fellow porters, while another is absorbed in his mobile device watching a Nepali movie.

Kristof from France joins me, as we had run into each other

during lunch. He was solo hiking for about 25 days through the region.

With his classic French accent he told me, "I love to hike alone. I can go as fast or as slow as I like. I stop when I want to stop. I hike when I want to hike."

He had his personal journal with him, as well as a French version of "The Snow Leopard."

We chatted a bit, but I told him I was capable of being quiet if he wanted to read.

He started working on his journal until dinner arrived at 6:30. We had both ordered dal bhat.

The previous night I had ordered pizza, and it was a poor choice. It was basically all doughy crust.

Brendan had asked how my pizza was.

"Great!" I didn't want to be a whiner.

When their meal arrived, it looked very tasty.

"Do you mind if I look at your food? What is it?"

They explained it was dal bhat, basically what the porters ate, and it was good. "Dal" translate to lentils and "bhat" to rice. The standard meal was composed of a lentil soup, rice, with either potatoes or vegetables served to the side.

"It's what we get every night. And it's basically all you can eat. They will bring you seconds, since they just make a large pot of the stuff."

"Well, I lied about my pizza being great. I want a do-over."
And I went ahead and ordered dal bhat. I asked Kaji if he
wanted my pizza and it disappeared.

I decided to call it an early night. At 10:30, I wake up long
enough to trim down to my woolies. I am toasty warm and
sleep well through the night.

I humbly await the trek to Lobuche. Getting closer to EBC!

To be continued.

Day 7 – Dingboche to Lobuche

November 22, 2014.

Day seven is the only day that I did not make journal entries while in the Himalayas. It wasn't because of a lack of memorable events.

I refer to this period as "the lost day."

Preferring an earlier start, I instead patiently waited for breakfast to be served. I figured this was a free subsidized meal for Kaji and I didn't want him to be short-changed.

I still remember the image of Kaji coming out of my room with my backpack on, a serious look on his face, his hearts beanie pulled over the top of his head, ready to take care of business. We had quite a hike ahead of us.

We start climbing the ridge we had climbed the day before. With Dingboche officially being 35 feet lower in elevation than Mount Whitney, we would now be above the highest point of the continental United States the rest of the way to Everest Base Camp. Very exciting!

I was pleasantly surprised that the climb to the top of the ridge seemed easier than the day before. My body was acclimatizing.

Reaching the crest of the hill, we could see miles to the northwest where we were about to travel. We dropped back down to a level path, and I was excited by the prospect of making good time along this unusually flat plateau.

A serious-looking Kaji prepares for the climb ahead. We start the day at about 14,500 feet.

Pheriche lies below us to the left as we hike to the NW.

Prior to today, we had been traveling basically northeast all the way from Tengboche to Dingboche, straight toward Mount Everest. We were now zigging to the northwest three miles to reach Dughla, then zagging back to the northeast again to head straight toward Lobuche, Gorak Shep and EBC.

On the southwestern edge of this extended plateau, to our left, there is a steep and significant drop down to the valley that contains the town of Pheriche. It appeared to me that Pheriche was quite a bit lower than Dingboche. Wouldn't it be easier to hike from Tengboche to Pheriche than to Dingboche?

Dingboche is at an elevation 14,470 feet. Pheriche is at 14,340 feet, which doesn't seem like that much of a difference. That being said, the route to Dingboche included a rise that needed to be crossed before dropping back down to the town.

Pictures can be deceptive. Having seen photos of this area before, I had thought the terrain looked kind of "boring," not very scenic. This wasn't the case at all. On both sides of this "fast lane" were monstrous and scenic mountains and vistas. Photos only capture a small portion of the view. It was a beautiful hike along this stretch. With the body utilizing less oxygen on this straight-away, it was even more enjoyable.

Right before reaching Dughla, we reach a semi-frozen stream that seemed to symbolize the arctic nature of the region. We stopped to take pictures before crossing a small bridge and climbing the rest of the way to Dughla.

Dughla is not a town. Well, it's not what I would consider a town. It consists of two lodges. But it is definitely at a crossroads. From here, you can head up to Lobuche, down to Dingboche and Pheriche or across the pass to Gokyo Lakes.

But it's the perfect place to have lunch on the way to Lobuche and that's what we did. There is a nice flat patio area outside of the lodges to soak up the unfiltered sun, but we chose to sit inside for the added warmth.

Right above Dughla is a large hill that needed to be climbed. I was intimidated from the start. In my mind, this was my own personal "Hamburger Hill." The angle was such that the whole mount could be seen. There was nothing left to the imagination. What you saw is what you got.

After lunch, we started climbing up the gradient. It was steep enough so that the first wave of exhaustion hit within 50 feet of elevation gain. Giminy, this was going to be tough. We were just starting and my heart was pounding like a jackhammer. I was already taking my first rest stop.

I had done so well climbing out of Dingboche, but this was different. We were climbing higher. The air was getting thinner.

The day would be separated into two parts, like "A Tale of Two Cities." The morning stroll was memorable and enjoyable. The afternoon would become memorable and miserable.

I felt like I was playing a video game. My RPG character's bonus stats were improving, but so were the corresponding challenges.

Frozen rapids right below Dughla.

Dughla is made up of two lodges at an elevation of 15,154 feet. The air is thin.

There weren't going to be any "gimmes" from this point on.

I looked at Kaji earnestly and said, "Let's be real about this." I figured it was coming sooner or later. Might as well make it sooner.

And I handed him my daypack.

And now I know what it feels like to be Catholic. I have confessed my shortcomings. And I judge myself to this day for that action.

He strapped the daypack on so that he was carrying it in front of his chest and we continued upward.

I pick out various large boulders on the path ahead to set myself micro-goals to reach. "Day-tight compartments," as Dale Carnegie would have said. All of the worries of tomorrow and the past can sink the strongest "ship," so only be concerned about the task that is immediately at hand.

I was now breaking my concerns down into 15-minute compartments.

About halfway up the mount, we encounter young porters hauling up oversized loads of construction lumber strapped to their backs. Their eyes conveyed something beyond exhaustion, beyond pain.

They were engaged in a personal battle to fend off despair.

"My God, my God, why have you forsaken me? Certainly, this isn't all that life has to offer. Certainly there is

141

Halfway up "Hamburger Hill" above Dughla.

Oh, the inhumanity! That's just too much!

something better around the next corner. There has to be." Their lives had come down to this one moment. Make it to the top of this hill or don't get paid. Do not pass go. Do not collect $10.

I had my camera at the ready, but used discretion. Reading the situation, I could tell they were not in the mood to have their suffering immortalized. I could envision the situation becoming violent if I utilized their struggle for my own personal Kodak moment.

*_*_*_*_*_*_*_*

In the past seven days, I had received great support through emails from friends and family.

At times, though, the internal cheerleaders fell silent, and it was necessary to plod onward like a mindless yak. Even then, I would remember the words of Ken Anderson. Some words just stick. They ring true to your heart and soul and you remember them for years to come.

I would dwell on his words and push forward to my next point of exhaustion, rest briefly, then begin again.

I first met Kenny when I was 18 years old and had moved up to Abilene to go to court reporting vocational school. I became a life-long friend with his older brother, Jerry Anderson, who I convinced to go to court reporting school so I could get $100 off my tuition. That was huge.

Kenny at the time was 15, a skinny, quiet kid. He never made any trouble and flew under the radar. I barely noticed him.

And somewhere along the years, skinny, little Kenny grew up. He not only grew up, he bulked up to inspirational proportions. He became somewhat of a superhero to me. Besides being incredibly disciplined with his bodybuilding, he engaged in a number of outdoor activities, including those on his ranch in central Texas. He also took up free diving and would dive to incredible depths with no oxygen tank, a feat that takes incredible mental and physical discipline, breaking through barriers of pain and panic. Scuba divers would freak out when they saw him and offer him oxygen, which he would just smile, shake his head and swim away. His photos of free diving with whale sharks in the Gulf of Mexico knocked my socks off.

And he even brews his own beer! Yep. Superhero status.

So even though he is just "little kid brother" to my lifelong friend, his encouragement was very meaningful to me.

 "If you don't reach Everest Base Camp, Karl, I am going to kick your ass."

--*-*-*-*-*-*

When we finally reach the top of the ridge, Kaji appeared under distress himself. This was a first. Sherpa are invincible, right? I was quite concerned and started thinking of what would happen if Kaji needed emergency evacuation.

"Kaji, how are you doing? I am worried about you."

He paused a moment, gathered his thoughts and replied stoically, "Sherpa are very strong people."

Kaji was one very tired and winded "strong Sherpa." To this day, I am indebted to him for helping me get up Hamburger Hill.

--*-*-*-*-*-*

At the top of this mount are a number of memorials to fallen Sherpa and Westerners who have died on Mount Everest, including a memorial to Scott Fisher.

There was still more climbing to do from here to Lobuche, and my fatigue continued. At one point I finally asked Kaji, "How much further?"

"About 20 minutes," he replied.

At that moment, 20 minutes seemed like an eternity. It brought absolutely no comfort. It extended beyond my five-minute compartments that I had now resorted to. This was a tough day.

We reached Lobuche and entered the lodge that Kaji had chosen for us. It appeared dark and dirty. I felt that I had gone back in time to a Wild West saloon of the mid 1800s. All of the gunslingers and ne'er-do-wells were casting me the evil eye as we walked in, warily eyeing up their competition. My mind filtered reality with an exhausted lens. In a seedy dive like this, no one of good character could be found.

I was shown to my room, traversing dark hallways to a dark and dirty room. It looked like the sheets had never been changed from the day they had first been put in the room. The top of the sheets was a darker shade of dirt than the

Pumori Peak graces our view heading northeast to Lobuche.

My mental health was challenged at Lobuche. This tent looked like a pleasant alternative to my lodging.

sides. The communal bathroom was a frightening place, with the floor wet and cold from leaking pipes. A row of sinks had a sign hanging in front of them reading "out of order."

Evidently, the pipes had frozen. There was no running water.

I went back to my room and peered out the window. Below the pane, the snow was stained yellow and brown.

My psychological health was on the precipice. I thought of Joseph Conrad's "Heart of Darkness." I was leaving civilization behind. I had reached the edge of the planet and I was about to fall into the abyss.

I went outside to get some fresh air where a European couple was sitting on a stone wall.

"The last time I was in a dump like this I was buying crack cocaine," I joked.

The lady laughed. The gentleman gave me a hateful glare. He wanted to hurt me.

I went further into the courtyard and had my picture taken next to a tent. On the previous portions of the trek, tent camping on the way to EBC had seemed absurd. Here, it appeared to be a pleasant alternative.

Dinnertime rolled around and I made small talk with the members of an organized, guided trek.

I asked Sam and Jessica during dinner, "How are you coping

with this?"

Jessica replies, "I can't. If I have to go to the bathroom, I just go outside."

After dinner, their trekking staff brought out a large plateful of fresh fruit, including sliced apples. Yum! It looked quite appetizing. And I am sure it was, but I was never offered a slice. It never crossed anybody's mind to offer me one. Oh, those silly, self-absorbed trekkers!

The fresh fruit taunted me, a mere two feet from my grasp. Eventually, the bounteous uneaten remains were cleared from the table. And that was that.

I went outside again to get some fresh air and to take a look at the stars. The cold immediately cut through all of my layers. I knew what the script called for. This was to be that special moment I went outside to admire the stars and take in the beauty of God's creation in awe and wonder.

But the cold was just too distracting to my senses. I looked up to the heavens and could make out but a few scattered stars. And before my eyes could adjust properly, I headed back inside to my dark and dirty room. The outside excursion wasn't quite the moment I had envisioned.

Inside my room, I laid out a plastic trash bag on one bed to protect my backpack and its contents there. My sleeping bag liner was then used underneath my sleeping bag to protect it from the questionable sheets.

My mental health was teetering. I was becoming despondent.

I crawled into my sleeping bag seeking escape by closing my eyes and listening to music on my iPad. I let the music transport me to another place.

My eyes started stinging from sweat and dirt and I couldn't think of anything clean enough to wipe my eyes with after seven days on the trail. Washcloth? No. Dirty. Towel? No. Dirty. Random articles of clothes? No. Dirty.

This was probably the lowest moment of my trip.

I got my eyedrops and carefully placed them in my eyes to alleviate the stinging. The near frozen drops were just one more assault to my senses.

And then a small revelation came to me. Tomorrow I was scheduled to reach Everest Base Camp.

I had completely forgotten. I was taking it one step at a time. I was truly living in day-tight compartments.

Finally, sleep came. Mercifully, the day ended.

To be continued.

--*-*-*-*-*-*

Day 8 – Lobuche to Gorak Shep and Beyond

November 23, 2014.

Kaji and I agree to meet at 6:30. I had given Kaji some snacks as a breakfast placebo, as I wanted to get a jumpstart and have plenty of time to make it to Gorak Shep. We are underway shortly.

It's very nippy this early and I stop shortly to exchange my windbreaker for my down jacket. I still have my soft-shell underneath.

It's about three hours to Gorak Shep, and I consistently forget how long that is at 5,000 meters.

Lobuche is 4,940 meters/16,210 feet. Gorak Shep is 5,180 meters/16,990 feet.

We have a view of Pumori a large portion of the way, a beautifully symmetrical peak shaped like a pyramid.

I take on and off my down jacket a few times before it stays on permanently for the rest of the day, along with my gloves. The cold wind is blowing.

There are a number of up-and-down rock scrambles on the way, and I think about the fact that the return trip will not all be downhill.

Having left at 6:45, we arrive at Gorak Shep by 9:30 and Kaji gets me checked into my room.

The room is acceptable, with only one bed, but there is a

Pumori graces our view to the north.

Continued climbing toward Gorak Shep.

shelf that I can place some things on.

I order vegetable soup and it is basically just broth. Maybe that is the best thing for me.

I am feeling the effects of the morning's climb and I lay down on the padded bench at the restaurant. I keep jerking awake from the cold.

Kaji says there is no hurry to head to Everest Base Camp, but by 10:30 I am ready to go.

I had mistakenly understood that this hike was a cakewalk. It wasn't.

The hike begins heading north through a flat and sandy dried-out lakebed. It looks like the future site of a Walmart store, just ready to be developed. It seems out of place and drab in comparison to the rest of the scenery.

We soon start climbing a ridge that follows along the western side of the Khumbu Glacier. What I hadn't previously realized is that the Khumbu Glacier is miles long. We had even been skirting its western edge before we reached Gorak Shep.

It is not the scene of the glacier that you see in the films above Everest Base Camp. The lower stretches are, for all practical purposes, stagnant. It's a dirty-looking combination of rocks, boulders, dust and ice. It's a forbidding-looking no-man's land that would be quite intimidating to explore.

When we are about an hour down the trail, I ask Kaji how

The alien landscape of the lower Khumbu Glacier extends way past Gorak Shep.

The Khumbu Glacier "proper" gets closer.

much further. I thought he would say 30 minutes. He said two hours. I was shocked. I was already pretty whipped.

I had read on the Internet, and mistakenly understood, it was a three-hour round-trip trek.

I was wrong. The Internet was wrong. It was two and a half to three hours each way, a significant difference at this stage of the game.

Although the route followed the western ridge of the Khumbu Glacier, there were still a number of significant ups and downs. The hike would not be over when we reached Everest Base Camp.

"Did you bring your headlamp?" I ask Kaji.

"No."

"Neither did I."

It was a bit of an extreme worry, but speaking from past experience...

I thought I had this in the bag, but I still had another grind in front of me, then behind me on the way back.

I went into short-sighted Mount Everest rookie climber mode. Don't worry about the trek back. Just get there. Every time the trail dipped down, then back up, though, I cringed.

Kaji waited for me as I took plenty of rest stops, as we were now trekking between 5,200 and 5,300 meters. Translated

Nuptse has been blocking our view of Mount Everest for most of the hike. Here, Nuptse is big and personal.

View north before dropping down to Everest Base Camp.

into terms that Americans like myself can easily relate to, that is between 17,056 to 17,384 feet. (Just multiply the meters by 3.28 to convert to feet. I finally had that number memorized.)

I developed a slight headache and slight nausea, both signs of high-altitude sickness.

Oh, no. Not now. I am too close. They were not severe and would come and go, so we carried on.

The scenery was spectacular. We crossed in front of Nuptse and Lhotse. The top of Mount Everest was visible midway through the trek, poking up above the Nuptse ridge.

We see the origin of the Khumbu Glacier off in the distance, the beautiful and dangerous icefall that we are more familiar with. It is impossibly far away.

Continuing to follow the ridge above the glacier, we finally drop down over 100 meters directly towards base camp.

Numbers flow very easily off the tongue when one isn't in the mountains and can lose their significance. This 100-meter drop was a huge commitment. A 100-meter drop means a 100-meter climb later in the day. Some trekkers are not willing to make this commitment and are satisfied with the view of Everest Base Camp from the top of this ridge.

Once at the bottom, we boulder skip and carefully navigate icier sections of the route down, around and then back up a small rise towards our goal. I was just following Kaji. It's quite a maze.

Kaji and I celebrate at Everest Base Camp, 17,598 feet.

There are also frozen lakes within the mass of the glacier, making for an other-worldly view.

We reach Everest Base Camp at 1:00 o'clock, two and a half hours after we started.

Kaji raises his hands in the air and I give him a high five. I absolutely could not have done it without him.

Achieving my long-held goal was met with relief, as much as any other emotion. This was just one moment of the adventure, a very symbolic part of it, yes, but also one of the cold, dirty and exhausted parts.

My thoughts were also swirling around the fact it was a long way back to Gorak Shep and I was exhausted and hungry.

We broke out the snacks and did our best to lighten Kaji's load.

I ask Kaji, "Did you know it was this hard?"

"Yes."

Kaji tells me, "You are very strong man." I tried to process what Kaji was telling me.

Kaji had carried my pack. I had gotten here because of Kaji's help. Kaji was strong.

On another level, I felt Kaji was trying to sincerely say that I had to be mentally tough to get through the struggles of the last eight days. Perseverance was needed. I had kept my focus. I had put one foot in front of the other in the right direction. I hadn't given up.

I was happy to accept his compliment in that context.

"Thanks, Kaji."

*_*_*_*_*_*_*_*

I was here. I was at Everest Base Camp. I was no longer in Kansas. I ran a diagnostic on my emotional state, looking for that ethereal moment of Zen.

It wasn't quite there. This would come later, I told myself.

And this was true.

Right now, I was still in expedition mode, planning my retreat back to Gorak Shep without blowing a fuse. I was constantly running ragged right beneath that point that would trip the breaker and the lights would go out.

I took in the view of the Khumbu Glacier. I had a deep respect for where I was and my surroundings. That being said, there was still a small, sardonic part of my psyche that viewed the Khumbu with an adversarial perspective. It was nothing of the "I beat the mountain" variety. No. The Khumbu still towered above me in command of its domain. But I felt the pride of a peasant boy who had snuck into the King's banquet hall and stolen a few crumbs of pastry. I had eluded the defenses thrown before me and I had my piece of the pie.

*_*_*_*_*_*_*_*

James, who I had previously met at Namche, shows up shortly after we arrive and asks, "How much further to Everest Base Camp?"

"You're there."

"Oh, cool!" And gives me a big hug.

"This is quite an achievement, especially for someone your age," James tells me. I just smile.

He tells me an American guide had just been throwing up from altitude sickness and lots of the trekkers were turning back.

James told me that Michelle and him were hanging out. (Michelle kept me company while climbing up to Namche.) They were going to meet somewhere that evening – and mentioned a name of a town I did not quite catch. That fact baffled me, as any town he might have mentioned had to be farther away than Gorak Shep. I just couldn't fathom the concept of hiking any further than the nearest lodge.

I offered him my snacks that were laid out.

"Oh, man, that's great. I haven't had Craisins in forever!" And the Craisins were gone.

Kaji and I take our mandatory pics, admired the view (there are so many to choose from) and we head back in reasonably quick order.

I remember to take a souvenir rock about fifty yards from base camp.

I was afraid Kaji would get upset but it's reasonably small and he even picks one out for me to choose from.

We then come back across a fossilized log I had seen off the trail earlier.

"Kaji, do you mind?"

"No. Go ahead."

I scramble slightly off the trail to search for a suitable specimen but I can't find something that "rocks my world." Most of the petrified wood samples I viewed were a bit "crumbly," not very solid, and I decide not to spend too much time looking. I save it for "next time."

I am totally whipped and take numerous rest breaks. I have been in the mountains enough times to know how my body reacts to stress. At a certain point, my body will just shut down, not even capable of generating heat.

We traverse back through the ups and downs on the ridge above the Khumbu Glacier. I am exhausted.

Other hikers are still coming toward EBC. I feel sorry for them. It's a tough hike.

Kaji is ready to get back. His pace is quicker than mine, but stops and waits for me each time he gets about 60 yards ahead of me.

My last "breath break" is about 12 feet from the lodge.

"Go ahead, Kaji. I can get it from here."

Kaji has tea waiting for me inside, but I can't get warm and start shivering. I don't go to my room because I figure it is colder there. I get a second cup of tea to little effect. I try to rest in the restaurant but I keep jerking awake from the cold.

I think tomato soup may do the trick, and it is as thin and watery as the vegetable soup. Fool me twice...

Around 4:30 Kaji comes around and I ask him when they are going to turn on the stove.

"I think it's on now."

I get up to go to the stove and am surprised how stiff and sore my legs are. That hadn't happened before on this trip.

The stove is burning and I attempt to warm myself up.

Dinner will be at 6:00 and I go to get my room organized. I start shivering right away and I get the feeling it's going to be the coldest night yet. I notice the blanket is the thinnest one yet, and I don't have a second blanket from a second bed.

I am a bit concerned, as I feel my body is not working at peak efficiency after pushing so hard to reach base camp, that it may not be able to generate the heat necessary to keep myself warm.

My strategy is to stay in the restaurant as long as possible that evening. A group of trekkers gathers around the stove and a worker tells them, "Go sit down. You are blocking the heat to the others."

With a chuckle they go sit down. I don't think they had ever been called "heat blockers" before.

Kaji notices my external power source for my iPad and asks to use it for his smart phone. It has an extra USB port and it worked great. He seemed very happy to be able to top off his battery.

I go up to my room and try to get organized for bed. I crawl into my sleeping bag with five layers on and hope I can get warm for the night.

To be continued.

Day 9 – Gorak Shep to Pangboche

"And if I shiver, please give me a blanket
Keep me warm, let me wear your coat."

"Behind Blue Eyes," by Peter Townsend

November 24, 2014.

It took a while, but I was finally warm enough to get to sleep. I doubled up the blanket, but that just caused it to slide off my slick sleeping bag.

I woke up around midnight and removed my down jacket, going down to four layers. It got down to 26 degrees that morning in my room.

I finally have my first clear dream since my arrival in Nepal.

My father pulls up in his pickup and offers to give me a ride out of the mountains.

"Thanks, dad!"

"You're welcome, son."

I wake up around 5:30 and drink from my half frozen bottle. I reach for the wet-wipes and they are frozen solid.

Kaji suggested we skip Kala Patthar and I was an easy sale. That would have required climbing up to 18,000 feet that morning. Instead, we would hike about six hours down to Pheriche. I was ready for an easy day.

We meet at the restaurant at 7:00 and we wait a bit for service. While waiting, I hand my glove to Kaji to see if he can fix it. I had pulled the liner out of place and couldn't get my fingers back in. It was just a mess.

Kaji and his friends pass it back and forth and, bingo, I have a glove again! That was a happy moment.

I order French toast and I am brought two types of jelly.

"Do you have honey, by chance?"

One of the gentlemen in the area grabs the honey and notices it is frozen in place. He holds it by the fireplace but decides that is not going to do it. He opens the stove and inserts the honey bottle. Shortly afterwards, I enjoy my French toast and honey.

I add that to my list of firsts, yak-dung-heated honey!

I tell Kaji that I am ready to go except I want to brush my teeth. He follows me up to my room as I brush and spit out the window. When I start to floss, he peers over my shoulder to get a better look. He is fascinated.

"It's an American thing."

It never dawns on me to put on a different dirty shirt or apply deodorant. I am in the zone.

We are underway at 8:00 and it is such a pleasure going downhill. Time takes on a completely different element.

It's kind of like having a steak dinner and not having to pay for it. (This being said from someone who has been meat free for the past nine days.)

"Say bye-bye to Gorak Shep!"

"Bye-bye!"

Not far out of town, he tells me in the spring this trail is covered with ice. It prods me to ask him, "How long have you been guiding?"

"For five years now. I started when I was 15. My father did this too, but he died when I was nine."

I start to slip and he turns around instantly and puts up both hands in case he needs to catch me. At that moment, I would give him the shirt off my back.

A bit further down the trail, I start dwelling on Kaji's comment about his father. And I remember the dream I had the night before.

--*-*-*-*-*-*

Mom was a country girl raised on a farm in South Texas. When I was a child, I would repeatedly ask mom to tell me "bedtime stories" about growing up in the country. I was fascinated with the subject.

When I was quite young, grandma and grandpa still lived on the property pretty much like they had when mom was a child. They lived in a simple home away from the main road reached by a sandy lane through the oak and mesquite. Grandpa still drove his Model T Ford. He would let me sit

166

behind the wheel as he shifted through the obstinate gears and we would drive down the sandy paths on the property. That was quite the adventure. I still remember him telling me, "The way you drive, a rattlesnake is going to crawl up and bite me on the neck."

This was very scary to hear and I thought there might be a rattlesnake in the back of the truck. I wasn't quite sure how my driving would produce such a result or what exactly he meant, but I still remember that to this day.

There was still no electricity to the farmhouse when I was a kid and it was very exciting spending the night and making one's way through the house by the light of the kerosene lantern.

Grandfather was a bit eccentric and on a number of occasions gave me advanced math lessons, drawing numbers and figures in the sand. For a young child, the lessons were quite intense. I almost comprehended some of the concepts.

Getting back to mom when she was a child, she would tend to the crops, milking the cows and other attendant chores that came along with the acreage. One of the stories that I still remember was about mom taking care of the pesky gophers on the property. The issue with these particular creatures was that they would dig holes in the ground, which theoretically could trip up a cow and break its leg. Mom was in charge of trapping these beasts. After trapping them, she would then beat them with a stick. For this service, she received two cents per deceased gopher.

Grandpa applied for a license to make wine from the grapes on the property, but big government thought better of it and a license was never granted.

But grandpa was an independent cuss. Mom and her sisters continued picking grapes for this clandestine activity, being handsomely rewarded with two cents for every pound of grapes gathered. This was not mom's favorite chore, though, as the wasps were zealous in defending their territory.

Mom would go on sales calls with grandpa, where free samples of wine were distributed and orders were taken. Grandpa's product was in demand. Business was brisk. You might say mom was a very successful assistant bootlegger.

In 1946, with mom's older sister taking the lead, mom left home at 16 and moved to the big city of San Antonio. She obtained employment at around $25 per week.

Dad grew up in Monroe, Michigan and joined the Air Force straight out of high school. He was immediately shipped down to Lackland Air Force Base for basic training.

This was not a traumatizing experience for dad. Dad was a track star in high school and nonchalantly went about basic training as an extension of his high school athletics. He was even able to put some weight on in the process.

Dad started attending church at one congregation while mom had followed big sister to another. Occasionally they would see each other in the ministry work downtown, where mom would tell her friend, "There is that silly soldier boy again."

After service work one day, dad invited mom to the fair downtown. They rode the Ferris wheel together and then he walked her home. And the rest is history.

On October 4, 1949, on dad's twenty-first birthday, they were married.

Soon after their wedding, they took their first picture together. Dad signed it, "To my sweetheart, always and forever."

Mom remained dad's sweetheart for the next 63 years.

Over the years, dad was pretty spoiled by mom. Dinner was served at 5:30 sharp. After his 8:00-to-5:00 workday, he was off duty while mom did the domestic chores. But he knew he was spoiled, so that makes it okay on many levels.

The situation changed when dad turned 82. Mom had a stroke that left her incapacitated. She was still sharp as a whip, but her ambulation was highly affected. When she recovered enough to come back home from therapy, dad surprised us all. He started washing dishes, doing some basic cooking and even learned how to do the laundry. He had really stepped up.

At 84, my father was checked into the hospital with advanced congestive heart failure. The cardiologist was at a loss. There was nothing he could do. Calling in a specialist, heart surgery was scheduled but it wasn't looking good. Mom went to see him for the last time at the hospital. As she left, dad blew her a kiss, telling her, "Always and forever."

We went home, resting ourselves for the recovery that was to come. He was transferred that evening to another hospital for the surgery. We got a call in the middle of the night telling us that dad passed away before it even began. The nurse on duty, who had just met father a few hours before, shed tears as she told us, "He wasn't concerned about himself. He just wanted to go home so he could take care of his wife."

At the cemetery south of town, just a few miles down the road from where mom grew up, dad was lowered into the ground at the end of the service. I asked my brother if he would be offended if I threw dirt on top of the casket. I wanted to assist in returning him to the earth from which he came.

I threw a shovel full of dirt on the casket and other family members joined in. His journey had come full circle.

"From dust we came and to dust we shall return."

As time passed, I didn't really dwell on his passing. Borrowing from my father's vernacular, he had a full life, as much as can be expected on this side of the Second Coming.

And life went on. I was at peace. I hadn't really thought of my dad much at all in the past few months.

And then with perfect clarity, dad was there in my dreams. Before that night, only static and confused images invaded my sleep, as if viewing an old black-and-white TV with a few bad tubes. My subconscious wasn't able to correlate and process all of the new imagery, all of the experiences being thrown at me in rapid succession.

"Dreaming dreams that don't make sense, even in the dream," was a notation I made on day six.

But this was different. In high-definition technicolor, I see the old Chevy coming up the trail. I am surprised to see dad when he pulls up beside me, but wasn't that just like him? I was no longer a child. He would no longer try to stop me from climbing that small dirt hill in Big Bend. He wouldn't try to stop me from trekking to Everest Base Camp. But get me out of the mountains as soon as possible? Yep. That's what dad would do. He would pull up in his old Chevy, tell me to hop in and then get the hell out of Dodge.

And then the idea hit me, what if it wasn't just a dream?

Here I was a little closer to heaven, within earshot, you might say, and he was just letting me know he still cared.

And things came to a halt for a while as the idea hit me. Kaji noticed my lack of forward progress and came back from down the trail, wanting to know what was wrong, if he had done something wrong.

I reassured him quickly, sharing with him that I just was thinking about my father and the dream that I had.

A couple of hikers passed by and inquired if I was okay.

"Yes, I'm fine. I just got a little dust in my eyes."

The moment passed, and then returned. Like the song "Ave Maria," the dream and this moment in my journey combined to hit a certain note that triggered an unstoppable emotional response.

I finally regained my composure, smiled at Kaji, smiled at the world and we continued down the trail.

Dad still loved me.

And it was a beautiful day in the Himalayas.

In loving memory of my father, Marion Avery Myers, October 4, 1928-January 10, 2013.

--*-*-*-*-*-*

I enjoy reminiscing on the way down and soaking in things I missed in my exhausted state on the way up. It was the best "rerun" I've ever viewed.

I turn around to enjoy the view of Pumori again. I notice for how many miles the Khumbu Glacier extends even past Gorak Shep. I enjoy again the wide tundra valley and hopping from stone to stone over the small, partially frozen creek.

We pass through forgettable Lobuche two hours later at 10:00.

We get back to the top of "Hamburger Hill" above Dhugla. We take a break to take more pictures of the memorials in the area.

On the way down, I tell a couple near the top, "I remember this hill."

They are in reasonably good spirits, perhaps because they are near the top.

"I bet it's a lot more fun going downhill."

On the way up, nobody ever made any comments about the luxury of going downhill, and I had decided to do the same.

"No comment."

From 10:45 to 11:20, we make it down Hamburger Hill to Dughla and have lunch.

Listening to my inner voice, I order a $3.50 Coke, my first one since learning of the yak tax. A silence descends over the patrons of the restaurant as I open the bottle and take my first drink.

The carbonation is amplified at this height and my chest is hit with a surge of taste and carbonation.

"Wow! That is powerful stuff!"

In my head, everyone stands up and cheers. A chorus line celebrates the event, sings and dances with confetti coming from the ceiling.

The emcee announces, "Coke! It will make you happy!"

I talk to Jess at the restaurant and he announces he is going 1.5 hours past my planned itinerary of Pheriche to Panboche.

Pangboche never made much of a mental impression on me because it wasn't on my stay-over list. I never even realized we had gone through the town. It was just kind of a wide spot on the trail.

From Dughla, there is the option to trek on the flat straightaway to Dingboche, but instead we drop steeply to the valley and head to Pheriche, which we could see far in the distance. I enjoy the new scenery, skipping over small creeks, viewing the yaks that run free in the valley. We stop to take pictures of a few of them, one enjoying scratching its neck against the shrubs.

We reach Pheriche and I was enticed by the appearance of many of the lodges, but it was only 1:30. I felt fresh and was ready to power on to Pangboche.

There was a bit of climbing involved on this portion of the trek and I was happy to pull into the lodge at 3:15.

We had dropped over 1,200 meters and the first small scraggly pines were beginning to appear again.

I have a private flush toilet and sink, but no shower. I ask for some hot water and rinse off a bit. Afterwards, I find out they have gas-powered hot showers for the asking. Argh!

Charging my iPad in the restaurant, a group of two women and one man are talking about all of the helicopter rescues in their group.

"We are all that's left." Three of their party have been rescued by helicopter for various altitude-related ailments.

They were on the same 12-day itinerary as myself. It's what the market wants (fast, fast, fast) but I feel strongly this hike would be much more enjoyable – and safe -- if another day was added in there somewhere.

A portion of the evening is spent corresponding with my travel agent Krishna about my itinerary. The word on the street is still that the Lukla airport will be closed this Thursday, November 27 for security reasons. Other trekkers have already gotten a jumpstart ahead of me, having made reservations for November 28.

He tells me I can charter a helicopter for $3,500. Goodness, I certainly hope it doesn't come to that.

To be continued.

--*-*-*-*-*-*

Day 10 – Pangboche to Namche Bazaar

November 25, 2014.

I sleep well through the night and get up to a brisk 39 degrees. Not too bad. It seems the other group slept well too. I think it's the lower altitude.

There is no running water in the sink, but that is certainly nothing to bother management about.

We get on the trail at about 8:15 and I try to get organized as to where we are.

Somewhere along the way, the path from Dingboche and the path from Pheriche converged and we were covering ground I had been on before.

"Do we still have to go through Tengboche?"

"Yes."

It started coming back to me as we approached the river in a wild canyon with Ama Dablam looming above in the early morning light at the end of the canyon. Surreal.

Deboche was just ahead after the river, where we spent night four. After Deboche, we climb back up to Tengboche. By 9:45, we reached the temple. It was great going down memory lane. The sun had come out and we put away our down jackets. That was the last time we wore them for hiking, although the soft-shell basically stayed on for the duration.

On the other side of Tengboche, we make our way down 500 meters, which had been a secondary test piece early in the trip.

Halfway down to the river, we took a break and the other group from the lodge did the same.

"Ever figure out how you are going to get home?"

"I have no idea."

I had asked Krishna just to book the next available flight after the airport reopened and he agreed that might be best.

The guide suggested a number of alternatives, including taking a helicopter to a town near Kathmandu and then take the bus from there.

Another suggestion was to get to Lukla by 11:00 the next morning and try to pick up a spare flight by happenstance.

That meant the plan was to hike past Namche today and hike at least to Monjo.

I wasn't happy with the prospect of bypassing Namche. Namche had a lot of creature comforts I had been looking forward to for a long time, mainly, a hot shower and clean environment.

(Plus the heating in the restaurant was supplied by an electric heater versus burning yak dung.)

All that aside, I thought that hiking late into the afternoon might be the best plan.

We reached the suspension bridge that traversed the river at the bottom of the valley at 11:20.

It had taken us three hours to make the journey from Namche to this bridge on day four and I figured it would be about the same coming back.

We still had to climb up from the river back to the heights of Namche, so the hike was no cakewalk.

About an hour before Namche, up on a high ridge, I saw a glint in the sun that appeared to be a small town.

"What town is that, Kaji?"

"Monjo."

"That's far away!"

"Yes."

I was a bit discouraged. I was ready to stop at Namche.

Once we reached Namche, we stopped at Kaji's sister's residence, where I met his sister and her husband. Kaji was planning to spend the night with them before continuing our journey.

Her husband threw down a cushion on their front step overlooking the city and we were served lemon tea.

Kaji's sister planned to go to Kathmandu for the winter. It was going to be too cold for them to stay.

Kaji was wrapping up his guiding season and he was heading home to mom's as soon as he got me safely to Lukla. It was a three days' walk from there. He planned to stay there for four months until the next trekking season.

We then hiked down to Namche Hotel, where I explained to Maya that I might need to keep hiking toward Lukla late that afternoon to see if I could catch an earlier flight before the closure on Thursday.

She explained with perfect conviction, "Oh, there is no need to do that because of blah blah blah."

I couldn't quite catch her reasoning, but at the same time, perhaps because my knees were acting as brakes all day, it sounded perfectly logical and I checked into a room.

Upon reading my emails, I found out that Krishna had booked a flight for me on Friday morning, just 24 hours later than originally planned, and I was pretty darned happy about that. I still had a chance to catch my international flight that afternoon.

I took my long-awaited hot shower and even decided to shave. Perhaps it was an excuse to stay in the hot water a bit longer.

Going back to the restaurant, Maya looked pleased.

"You look much better now."

I recovered my plastic bag that I left behind on day four and rummaged through it to see what we could dispose of. Kaji left with the big jar of almond butter and a few cans of tuna to his sister's. I also gave him the pair of over-gloves I had picked up earlier, so he would have a chance to give them to his sister or take to mom's.

There were Buddhist monks chanting in the room next to the dining hall. There was a pretty consistent beating of drums and an occasional blowing of a horn.

Miss Prissy, dining a few feet from them, didn't seem to enjoy that very much.

Maya was hosting the monks for some occasion. Every so often, goodies would be brought in, including a tray of cookies.

I was very happy to be in Namche. I turned in early, turned on the electric blanket and snuggled in. I thought it was best to set the alarm in case I overslept in the morning. There were no discomforts to act as an alarm clock.

I slept until the alarm went off.

To be continued. I'm not home yet.

*_*_*_*_*_*_*_*

Day 11 – Namche Bazaar to Lukla

November 26, 2014.

It seemed quite uncivilized that I had to hike one more day after having settled into the comforts of the Namche Hotel.

Kaji came by and said Chhiring Sherpa's wife wanted to see us before we left.

"Do you know why?"

"She just wants to see you."

Kaji is going straight to mom's house for the winter, so his daypack is a bit bigger than usual, but he still manages to jam it into my pack. I knew this was coming and put all of my bulky jackets into my own daypack.

We leave the hotel and hike uphill. Kaji leaves my backpack on the ledge outside by the walkway and he motions me upstairs. I guess there are no thieves in Namche, I uncomfortably try to reassure myself.

Yangee serves Sherpa tea as her little girl practices her English, then settles into watching Nepali cartoons.

We politely turned down second helpings. Yangee then brings out a Kota and wraps it around my neck.

"For good luck."

I thanked her, and then turned to Kaji, "Do I keep this?"

Trail just below Namche Bazaar.

This viewpoint one hour below Namche Bazaar is the first and last glimpse of Mount Everest you will get on the trail.

We give our goodbyes and go outside, with this long scarf still around my neck.

"Can I take it off now?"

"Yes." He puts it in my pack and we start our hike at around 8:15.

A bit down the trail, a yak train is coming, so I start making my way off the trail, stepping in front of a middle-aged German couple.

The fräulein, noticing I am between them and the yaks, says, "Ya, I like you right there."

I laugh and climb a bit further off the trail.

The fräulein looks at me with disdain. "Ah, so you are scared, are you?"

I just laugh. "No, just respectful."

After tying the Kota to the first suspension bridge, we continue to cross, but a porter with a large load of San Miguel beer approaches. It is about four feet wide, so I go to the side of the bridge and start leaning over to get out of his way. Then lean a little bit further. The San Miguel beer must flow!

At the second suspension bridge, a long train of mules is coming across so we take our packs off to take a break. One of the first mules gets its pack stuck on the chain-link fence and all kinds of chaos breaks loose. Despite its best efforts, it could not break free. The mules behind start piling up. Everyone on our end didn't want to go out onto the bridge and deal with a panicked mule. The mule finally frees itself, but it was quite a situation.

While waiting out the rest of the train, Meg, a student from Washington, D.C., starts chatting with Kaji in Nepali. I had already pulled out the snacks and offered her some.

"No, thanks. But I have a not too overly ripe apple, if you want it."

I hadn't had fruit in over a week.

"Uh, okay."

"It's not too overly ripe," she repeated, "but I just can't deal with it."

"Well, how 'overly ripe' something is depends on how long you've been in the mountains."

It tasted pretty good.

She asks where I have been and I tell her I have been to Everest Base Camp.

"I hear that's nothing but a -- pile of rocks."

I thought to myself, did she just say "f---ing"?

"Well, it's a symbolic pile of rocks."

"Yeah, I guess so."

At about the same time, we hook up with a Nepali guide and his two Irish clients. Boy, did they have a thick brogue.

Kaji and the Nepali guide start engaging in a deep conversation.

Kaji tells me, "Go ahead. I will catch up." And Kaji and the other guide stop to have an in-depth discussion, about something.

I am also lost in conversation talking to one of the Irishmen about his trip to Yosemite and his thoughts on Half Dome when another train of mules come up and...

"Gentlemen," I announce, "we are on the wrong side of the trail."

We had violated the golden rule. We had allowed the mules

to walk along the face of the cliff and we were lined up along the abyss. I look straight down, realizing if one of these beasts bumps me, I am Post Toasties.

I remain calm, as there was nothing else to do. Actually, there was, but I won't get into what set off a yak stampede earlier in the trip.

The mules remained calm, we remained calm, and it all worked out. But I thought to myself, Kaji leaves me for five minutes and I almost kill myself.

We stop to have lunch at Phakding with the Irishmen and their guide. I wanted to confirm with them that our guides were getting compensated for their dinners for taking us to certain lodges and restaurants. Which was great, as I didn't want Kaji spending money out of pocket.

"Yeah, the guides get taken care of, but the porters are on their own."

That's when I noticed the Irishmen's porter slumped in a corner of the courtyard, arms crossed, looking sad and hungry. That wasn't so great.

We take off from Phakding with about three hours to go to Lukla. The clouds had blown in and we walked uphill into the clouds and dampness.

Arriving at Lukla a bit before 4:30, we walked through town for perhaps a kilometer. This portion of Lukla consisted of a single lane cobbled with stone. The sides of the lane were enclosed by shops and houses also consisting of stone and mortar, giving it a claustrophobic and medieval appearance.

The overcast weather helped add to this mental imagery.

Dogs were fighting. Dogs were puking.

If I arrived by air on a clear and sunny day, I am sure the town would have had a different first impression on me.

We walk around the edge of the airport and we come to the Buddha Hotel.

"You, stay here."

"Right here?"

The weather definitely affects the mood and the ambiance of Lukla. This is the main corridor through the town. The trail horseshoes up, over and back down on the other side of the airport.

"Yes."

So I stand motionless outside the door as Kaji goes inside. I thought he wanted to conduct the check-in business by himself.

He looks at me quizzically and motions me to follow him.

"You stay here tonight." Oh. Okay.

The location is good. I am right next to the airport and can see what is going on and not going on.

Kaji obtains a key to the room, but I don't know from whom. We sit down on the bed getting situated and a five-year-old boy runs into the room and starts messing with my iPad. Kaji physically grabs him and throws him out of my room.

Shortly after, he enters the room again, crawls over my stuff and grabs my altimeter. Kaji gets a bit more forceful and hauls him out of the room and this time we lock the door.

Soon after, he appears on my windowsill and is banging on the window. I ignore him. I saw the movie "Let Me In," about a child vampire, and I knew better.

We are on the third floor and he is on the one-foot sill. I am a little freaked out by this, but I am not going to encourage him. It's not cute anymore, if it ever was.

When we get up to leave, the exit from our hallway is locked. The wild child of Lukla was not happy with the situation and had locked both us and another pair of guests in the hallway. After a few minutes of knocking, the door was finally unlocked.

Wanting to obtain Internet, Kaji accompanies me to the registration desk, where there is nobody in sight. The registration area/restaurant is dark and unlit at the moment. There is one individual sitting near the stove and slurping noodles, but I don't know who he is. Eventually, a twelve-year-old girl appears and hands me a liter of water, which I had previously requested.

"Kaji, how much is this place?"

After a few interactions with the gentleman at the stove, he ceases his slurping noises long enough to announce, "1,000." One thousand rupees being about $10.

I still have no idea if this individual works here or if he just knows the price of the hotel. He continues sucking up the last of his noodles.

"How about Internet?"

Kaji replies, "No Internet tonight. Maybe tomorrow."

Somewhere in all of this, I ask Kaji if he can help retrieve my bag I had transported here about ten days ago. I assumed it was at this same hotel. He calls Chhiring and finds out it is at another hotel. Kaji goes to retrieve it for me. Highly appreciated.

Kaji tells me it's time for him to take off. I give him my headlamp and a tip that probably equaled what he received for his guiding services. He gives me a Kota and a hug. Now I just need to find a bridge to tie it to.

We exchange phone numbers and emails, just in case, and Kaji is gone.

From past experience, I figure I should try to take a shower ASAP, before it gets even colder that evening. There has been no heat in any of the lodges I have stayed in.
I let the water run for about five minutes. I can feel a slight hint of lukewarm-ness and figure I am getting close so I step into the shower and it doesn't feel lukewarm. It was ice cold. My mind had been playing tricks on me. I splash the front of my body with a bit of cold water but I am not willing to commit the other half.

Civilization, so close, yet so far away.

I head back up to the restaurant/registration area and some of the lights are now on. Now it only halfway resembles a hobbit hole. I park in front of the wood-burning stove (I'm moving up in the world) and hang out, not seeing anyone who acts like they work here, but a few guys do hang out by the stove, munch on snacks loudly and talk loudly.

No one has acknowledged my presence. No one I have seen acts like they work here. I get the impression I have barged into someone's home and they are just coping with that fact.

Kaji had already ordered dinner so I wait to see what happens. Eventually, a young man with a thin mustache brings out my veggie pizza. I eventually work up enough nerve to approach the men back at the stove.

"Is there any way I can get Internet tonight?"

"No Internet tonight. No Internet in all of Lukla." Later I

confirm this is true. At the time, though...

Later, they give me a password to the Internet, "just in case"
it comes back online. It's a long series of numbers, and with
their heavy accents, and the two men tag teaming the
numbers to me, I was concerned I would not get the
numbers right and I would have to bother them again. I
didn't want to bother them again.

I could tell I was hooked up to their Internet at the lodge, but
they were not hooked up to the greater Internet.

A couple of younger girls brought dinner to another table,
giggled and then disappeared for the evening.

Pretty soon I was the only one left in the restaurant that
appeared to be a guest, so I head back to my room. It was
cold in there, so I head back up to the stove in the restaurant.
I felt as though they were tolerant of me, even though I had
barged into their space. I appreciated that fact. I finally
work up the nerve to ask the gentleman with the thin
mustache for some hot tea. Now, it's one thing to just barge
into someone's home, but then to ask for refreshment too? I
felt like a real s---.

When I head back to the room, it was cold. I am cold. I feel
like I have paid my dues. Why do I still have to be cold?
I crawl into my sleeping bag with my usual four layers (no
poly layer. I like the feel of the Merino wool) and start
working on my journal. I fall asleep sitting up in bed.

To be continued.

--*-*-*-*-*-*

Day 12 – Stranded in Lukla

November 27, 2014.

I wake up to the sound of a helicopter warming up. With my room being strategically placed right next to the airport, I wipe off the condensation from the window and see it take off.

A number of helicopters take off into the fog but no airplanes. Okay. At least I am on the right page. I am not the only one stranded here. My original ticket was for this morning.

I see the doorknob turn to my room and I don't think a thing about it. It's probably just a vampire looking for permission to enter and claim my soul or some other such frivolity.

"Can I help you?"

A helicopter is taking off so I can't hear the reply.

A bit later there is a knock and I again ask who it is.

It is Kaji.

He comes in and explains he is going to try to take a plane today so he only has to walk one day to mom's house. Evidently, he had walked far enough lately and had a happy tip in his pocket.

That was certainly understandable.

He takes the curtains to wipe off the condensate from the

View from Buddha Lodge. In an effort to prevent planes from flying into the sides of mountains, days' worth of flights are often canceled.

windows so we have a better view. What a brilliant idea!

We go out for coffee and apple pie at the German bakery right next to the airport.

Since we are right there at the departure entry, I go in to see what is happening. Overall, there is not much going on.

All of the counters are empty except one, and I have already decided I am not going to be pushy. If I can obtain information, I will. If not, so be it.

I thought I saw Meg sitting on the floor chatting, and I remembered in the back of my mind she mentioned the earliest two flights would still take off. But it was way past 7:30, when she said her flight was scheduled, so I didn't think much about it.

I went back up to my room and at 10:30, a plane landed. A few minutes later, another plane landed, then another.

A few minutes later, planes were taking off.

I was a bit nervous and went back to the airport to investigate.

I saw a couple of approachable European women and asked what was going on.

"We are flying to Kathmandu." This was after about four planes had taken off.

"But I thought no one was flying to Kathmandu."

"They aren't, but our agent was able to arrange it special for us. We were going to take a helicopter and now two seats are open on that. Maybe you can get on."

They were very sincere in trying to help and sympathetic in that they knew I didn't know what was going on. They pointed to someone who was assisting them and said, "Please help this gentleman if you can."

He kind of shrugged his shoulder and said if anything came up, he would let me know.

After these flights took off, the airport was completely empty. No one was behind the counters to ask questions.

The weather on arrival to Lukla. Planes had taken off just a few hours before.

Yaks line up to be loaded by the Lukla Airport.

Earlier, there was one counter with an attendant, but as soon as he helped the people in front of him, he took off down the hallway into the administrative offices.

I wanted to confirm that the ticket that I had on my iPad was still valid but there was no one to talk to.

I sat in a chair by myself waiting for something serendipitous to happen for about an hour in the empty airport lobby.

It didn't.

Another young couple came in and said they were catching a flight to Jiri. From there they would hire a jeep to take them to Kathmandu.

They told me they had a ticket for tomorrow to Kathmandu and that it was canceled.

"That's what I was afraid of." I had a ticket for tomorrow also, but in Nepal, I wasn't sure what that meant.

"Yeah, I am just hanging out waiting for something surrendep -- serendep -- "

"Serendipity?"

"Yeah. I have trouble with that word."

And then it dawned on me. I hadn't saved a snapshot of the email showing my new ticket number, airline, time of takeoff, etc.

And the Internet was down across Lukla. I couldn't retrieve the email and a copy of the ticket.

Oh, crap. What am I doing?

I go back to the German bakery and the Nepali working there was super helpful. He attempted to call Krishna so I could receive the information.

There was only one problem. The lines were not operational at the time.

I started wandering around looking for Internet that worked. I walked into a very presentable lodge. They were kind enough to inform me that the Internet was truly down across Lukla.

Then it dawned on me. I didn't necessarily need to have the Internet to retrieve old emails. I looked in my received folder and found a copy of the ticket.

Deep sigh. I am making progress.

I go back to the airport and it is still empty. Deciding it was time to be a bit more forward I wander down a side corridor into the private offices back there.

Someone in a small office associated with Tara offered assistance. "Thanks, but I have a ticket for Yeti."

"No, it's Tara. Yeti and Tara are the same airline."

They said the ticketing office was on the other side of the airport and would open at 2:00.

And then another vague memory came to me. Meg mentioned if you didn't check in the day before, they would cancel your ticket. That's why she was in such a hurry to get to Lukla and didn't stop for lunch.

I then realized if I hadn't been putting in all of this effort to double-check the validity of my ticket, it could have been canceled on me. Scary!

Paranoia sometimes can be a good quality!

I go to the other side of the airport and find a coffeehouse with wifi. A young lady named Nima has been left in charge and brings me multiple cups of coffee and hot tea.

Wow! Things are getting good.

At 2:00, I go to the only official-looking structure on the side of the airport indicated to me and a guard quickly blocks my entry and points to the other side of the airport for ticketing.

Frank from Canada was just walking by and said, "Hey, I am going to the same place. Follow me."

So I do.

We take the trail up and over to the other side of the airport by my lodge. Without pause, Frank walks into the admin area. Without pause, they tell us the ticketing is on the other side of the airport.

"They open at 3:00."

"Uh, could you point to us exactly where this place is?"
He points in the general direction of the "other side."

"Uh, can you describe it? What color?" I couldn't seem to
find it previously.

He is good enough to take a snapshot and then blow it up of
what the building looked like. I didn't get a good view.

Frank acts like he understands where it is. We again take
the trail up, over and down to the other side of the airport
and he keeps walking into town.

"I thought it was right next to the airport."

He keeps walking deeper and deeper into town and there is a
big two-story structure with a large sign that says "XX
Lodge" and a very small sign that says "Tara."

I never had a clue. Good job, Frank!

The counters are, of course, empty. But soon enough, an
assistant comes and looks at my iPad ticket. He looks
through a sheaf of papers and puts a check mark by what I
assume is my name.

That check mark was very reassuring.

"What hotel are you staying at?"

"Buddha Lodge."

"Okay. We will call your hotel if there is a delay."

"Wow. Nice service," I wrote in my journal, as if I believed they would actually take the effort to track me down.

I go back to the coffeehouse to use the Internet until about 4:00, then decide I should start getting my thoughts together back at the hotel.

Near the top of my to-do list was to obtain a shower before my 30-hour international flight. It just seemed like the right thing to do.

In my mind, I tried to formulate a strategy to make this a reality. I just couldn't figure it out. In the past, I have created Excel spreadsheets that took less brainpower.

Heading back up to my room at Buddha Lodge, there is a lone figure in the dark stairwell. I ask him, "Is there any way I can get a shower around here?"

The visage turns towards me, stares right through me and in a scary ghostlike voice intones, "Guestttttt, showerrrrrr."

I think to myself, uh, yes, the guest does want to take a shower. Thank you for that clarification.

Back at the room, I confirm the water is still cold.

I go back up to the restaurant to ask if there is any hot water.

There has got to be hot water in Lukla. I just know it.

The person I ask points to the other side of the restaurant. I follow the direction he is pointing. It leads to one person who looks like he is not working by the stove and then another person directly behind him who looks like he is not working watching someone play video games.

I stop next to the person by the stove, look back to the person who is giving me direction. I point directly at the person by the stove questioningly. He shakes his head and indicates further down.

I then proceed to the person watching the computer screen of the individual playing computer games.

"Is there any way to get hot water for a hot shower?"

"In guest shower. Follow -- "

He stops mid-sentence and screams in excitement, following the action on the computer screen.

When the excitement on the screen subsides, he continues. "Follow little boy. He show you."

First thought. I think back to the ghostly visage I had seen earlier. It was not, "Guesttttt, showerrrrr." It was, "Guesttttt showerrrrr!"

Ah, the mysteries of Lukla!

Second thought. Having figured this out, I mentally scold myself for making such an absurd assumption that showers in the rooms were actually there for taking showers. If you want a hot shower, you ask to use the "guest shower."

Third thought -- oh, I don't know. I will leave it at that. I follow the little eight-year-old boy down the stairs. He turns the light on so we can see better.

No, no, no. Don't do that. It makes it too easy!

He goes to the end of the hallway and shows me the guest shower.

He starts demonstrating how to turn the nine knobs that are there, and I know the odds that I will be able to figure this out later after he leaves are miniscule.

There was a heating unit on the wall right there in the bathroom, and I was somewhat familiar with such devices from Thailand, but there were just too many knobs.

I go back to my room and burn more brain cells trying to figure out what to bring and what not to bring.

Going back to the guest shower, I start playing with the knobs. I try to stand behind the door leading into the shower room while doing this, but my soft-shell and the only pair of pants I have for the trip begin to get soaked from the splattering water. And the water is still cold.

I give up. I go back up two flights to get assistance.

The gentleman takes leave of watching the video game and goes downstairs to assist.

After a reasonable period of time, he places the white bucket that was in the corner under the flowing water to stop the splattering. Smart!

He finally gets the algorithmic formula down where it seems

I could never figure out how to create hot water from all of these knobs. Grrrrr!

to be the right temperature and he takes off.

I place most of my clothes outside of the shower room so they don't get wet. The water is still colder than I want it to be and I never get comfortable. I work around to getting my backside wet this time, though.

I knew which knob was hot and which was cold, but it appeared the cold was already all the way off, so that didn't solve things.

I tried slowing the water flow on the hot side to very little effect. (That could theoretically give the water more time to heat while flowing through the heating unit.) The rest of the knobs were too big of a mystery to mess with. I didn't want to jump from the frying pan into the fire. Or the frying pan into the cold water.

I turn off the water and reach outside of the shower room to grab the towel. Then again to grab my soft-shell top. Then my pants. I hop around a bit trying not to drag the pant legs on the wet floor.

To grade my performance above a C would be too kind.

*_*_*_*_*_*_*_*

I have figured out that the staff appreciates it if you place your dinner order ahead of time, so I poke my head into the kitchen where I had been directed.

I saw what appeared to be a family unit working around the fire-burning stove and a table full of chopped vegetables and potatoes. My attitude softened toward "management." That being said, just a minimal amount of training in communication skills would make a huge difference in the enjoyment of their guests' stays.

I ordered a veggie spring roll. It seemed like a good choice. It was fried for safety and had veggies. Perfect compromise. It was actually quite tasty.

Oh, yes. Happy Thanksgiving! I had almost forgotten.

Was my ticket valid? Would the weather worsen and flights be canceled? How could I reach United to cancel my ticket? Would I lose its value if I can't reach them? Would they put me on the next available flight if the puddle jumper is running late? So should I even try to cancel?

Tonight, though, I am hopeful that my flight plans will materialize and I will make my international flight.

Don't call it serendipity. Don't call it a good attitude.

Call it watching the little commuter planes fly off into the thick, gray, impenetrable fog today and not being able to imagine the weather getting any worse.

To be continued.

Day 13 – Stranded in Lukla

The following was my complete initial journal entry for Day 13, November 28, 2016:

Not a single plane flew in or out of Lukla.
United says they will try to rebook once I get to KTM.
I have been told I am set for 7:00 a.m. tomorrow, weather permitting.
There was a nice German pastry shop I hung out at for most of the day, so that helped.
Best to everybody!

--*-*-*-*-*-*

Stranded in Lukla – Day 2. The longer version.

It took eight days to reach EBC, three days to walk to Lukla, and now this was my second day attempting to leave Lukla.

Noting the lack of activity at the airport, I asked Tara personnel, "I know the planes are delayed, but do you think we will get out today?"

"Oh, yes, yes." So the day was spent first in the airport lobby, watching our breath dissipate in the cold air, before moving headquarters to the German bakery.

I never had a "hard" ticket during any of this time, but would display my iPad to the officials when trying to get information.

After waiting all day for the weather to clear, I heard through the grapevine I should re-report to the Tara Airline office in town to be reissued -- something. It wasn't a ticket. To get back "on the list," I guess.

I walk down the one stone-and-dirt lane to the Tara office and wait patiently in line.

"Show up at 7:00 tomorrow."

That's it. No more information. No less.

I had begun to hear disturbing rumors that it could take weeks to get a plane out of Lukla.

On the way back, I stopped at Illy's Coffee House for Internet and refreshment. I saw a sign on the wall mentioning they provided helicopter service.

I inquired with Nima about costs. She got ahold of "uncle," who also owned the coffee shop, with a $500 price quoted. The price began to seem more and more reasonable the more I thought about it.

Since I am all packed up ready to go wherever I want, I decided to check out and check in to the Himalaya Lodge above the airport. From here, I could still see clearly the airport. It looked nice from the curb.

I walked in and asked about prices. She showed me a price list with different options.

"Do you have any private rooms with hot showers?"

"Yes, but that's $15." I hesitated for about two seconds looking over the room menu.

The Himalaya Lodge is located right above the airport.

Feeling a bit wild and crazy? Got a spare $10? Then you too can get a room with a gas-powered hot shower in Lukla.

"But for you, $10."

"Deal."

I am shown to my room, which has a sliding deadbolt attached between the two swinging doors. The four screws are coming out on the side that has the eye for the bolt. I handle the bolting procedure gingerly so that it doesn't completely fall off.

I am not concerned of anyone breaking into my room. It's too cold for such nonsense.

Realizing the lodges are highly subsidized by their meals, I order dinner there. A couple I had been hanging out with all day also took my suggestion to try out this lodge.

As usual, when they got their meal, I asked if I could check it out.

She got a potato pancake with cheese on top and he got what almost looked like veggie spaghetti but he said was more like chow mein. Both meals looked quite edible.

I ordered a chapati with scrambled egg, as I planned to make a giant taco out of it. It would help remind me of home. I also ordered Sherpa stew, the vegetarian variety.

Frank, who I had run into in Lukla while looking for the ticket office, casually informed me how he had been eating meat on the trip and had only gotten seriously ill once.

"Yeah, I was just puking up big chunks of chicken." Like it wasn't a thing.

If anyone asked, his first choice of dining was the hotdog place down Lukla Row.

I had my usual four layers on in the lodge and thought management was being a little cheap with the yak dung. I wasn't that sociable and just sat to the side charging my electronics.

Before when I was cold and lonely, there was a purpose. Now I am just waiting. I'm ready to go home.

I didn't look forward to going to my even colder and darker room. Even the hot shower brought little comfort. Eventually, that water had to be turned off.

It was a gas-powered shower, and it was easier to figure out as I could see the outline of the gas flames increase as I turned a certain knob a certain way.

I slept with my head at the foot of the bed, which was closer to an electrical outlet, so I could still charge my iPad and listen to music with my headphones.

The walls here were thin. I could hear a couple chatting a bit through the walls, and I didn't mind. It was my closest link to humanity and the outside world.

*_*_*_*_*_*_*_*

Day 14 – Escape from Lukla

November 29, 2014.

I wake up early. I am too nervous to think about breakfast. My scheduled international flight left yesterday and things are nebulous.

I head down to the airport with my duffel bag and small carry-ons.

There is hope. I can clearly see the mountains above, off and on. The question is, what is the weather like in the valley below?

That didn't seem overly promising.

I wait in the Tara office at the airport. My "verbal ticket" is the gentleman on the other side of town saying "Show up at 7:00."

Frank is even more excited. He paid cash at the Tara office and got a small slip of paper that had "7:00 o'clock" written on it.

From 6:45 to 7:15 I stand at the counter in the Tara office and I am professionally ignored. My presence is not acknowledged. Situations like this make time slow down. Kind of like when you are hiking above 5,000 meters. It's quite comparable.

The office staff is mute when it comes to inquiry.

One young Japanese fellow walks in and stands behind me.

Partly cloudy. Partly sunny. Maybe a flight. Maybe not a flight. Who knows?

I tell him, "Have at it."

"Can I get a ticket for a flight today?"

The lady in the back actually breaks her silence.

"No!" She returns to her paperwork.

One gentleman was popping in and out of the office on different occasions. He demonstrated a dash of humanity and was kind enough to inform us, "We are waiting for the guy from the other office to bring the papers."

That was helpful.

Frank is beginning to get rowdy, and the same gentleman offers him the phone to talk to the guy from the other Tara office "with the papers."

I am still in "not rowdy mode," and around 7:15, the helpful gentleman walks in again, gives me a slightly sympathetic glance, speaks to another office staff member and points directly at me before walking out.

The other staff member picks up a sheaf of paper from the desk and walks over to me. "You're number eight."

Frank, you're on your own. I'm number eight.

I walk out into the airport lobby and what I see in the lobby is disconcerting. In my journal, I used the word "frightening." Other passengers seem to know what is going on. Large groups walk into the airport lobby in lockstep and proceed forward with conviction. Others are checking baggage through to the other side of security.

This is one of the benefits of being part of a larger tour group. Assistance and guidance in getting in and out of Lukla can be priceless.

I walk up to a small group who appears to have a Nepali guide with them.

"What is going on? I don't have a clue."

I still don't have a ticket. All I know is that I am "number eight."

I am informed the Tara planes will come in groups of four.

The first four planeloads were getting ready to take off, even though there were no planes that had come from Kathmandu.

"Won't I need a ticket to get through security?"

"Nah."

I go back to the German bakery and get the last piece of apple pie. The last piece always tastes best.

A couple I hadn't seen before were quite cheery.

The young lady with enthusiasm and bravado announced, "Oh, I'm sure it's all going to work out."

I was unmoved. "I've been through the African campaign, I'm heading to Italy and I no longer have faith." I was a jaded veteran and no longer believed in this mythical creature called a "plane" in Lukla.

Poking my head out one more time and viewing the fog in the valley, I made my decision. I'm getting a helicopter.

I informed a couple of gentlemen who had hung out in the bakery with me the day before of my decision and I take off to Illy's.

About 15 minutes later, they joined me.

When a couple of young Asian girls at the coffeehouse saw what was happening, they asked, "Can we get a helicopter too?"

I felt I was beating the rush.

Previously, I had asked Nima's uncle if he took credit cards for the helicopter flights. When he said yes, I didn't realize that meant going to the "money man" next door, who was going to charge ten percent to run my card through and hand me $500 in cash.

Ah, well. In for a penny...

After the credit slip was signed for $550, I was handed my $500 in cash, which I then promptly handed over to the waiting Illy man.

The older gentleman grabbed one side of my duffel bag, I

A helicopter in the hand is worth more than a few nebulous airplane reservations in Lukla.

grabbed the other and off we go to the "heli field."
"Heliport" would be pushing it.

In a bit, I am split off from the two gentlemen who followed me over and I am taken to a lonely field on the other side of the airport. Another couple that had joined us for this journey are a bit freaked out by this. For all they know, they have just given someone $1,000 and they got a great tour of an empty field.

It's explained that two helicopters are coming at once and they need the space.

The helicopter comes in reasonably prompt order and there is a bit of commotion. My carry-on is taken to the other side of the heli for storage as we are rushed to the other side of the helicopter. I notice among the baggage being unloaded is a carry-on that looks suspiciously like mine.

I go over, open up the top zipper and notice a Ziploc bag that looks suspiciously like mine.

Close enough. I'm taking it. Upon further examination, I confirm it was my bag.

We take off and head toward Kathmandu. At one point I hear something that sounds suspiciously like a stutter as we skew slightly to one side. He is trying to gain altitude to get through the next pass in the mountains.

We make it! Oh, joy!

(I hear from Krishna later that day that four planes escape Lukla. Does that mean I would have been number four on

Sunday? No idea. My Lukla math isn't that good.)

At the Kathmandu airport, I request assistance from someone with a trolley to help transport my gear from the domestic to the international terminal.

Before I know it, three people are assisting, two having grabbed bags off the trolley.

At first, I think, whatever. I can spare an extra few dollars. But then it dawns on me, if they start running in opposite directions, I'm screwed.

At one point, I lose track of my small backpack with my passport in it. It's not a good feeling and I feel a bit panicky. I grab it from him and give him $1. He didn't want to give it up. Too bad. I never needed your help anyway.

At the dirt hump, the duffel bag comes off the trolley and the one young man is earning his keep by carrying it.

Now I am down to two guys, when I only needed one.

I give the young man carrying my duffel bag a tip, which was probably equivalent to a day's wage in much of Nepal. "Split it with your friend however you want."

"You think this is a good tip? We walked a long ways."

I instantly flash back to Illy's Coffeehouse where a young trekker was talking about the unpleasantness he encountered in India. No matter how big of a tip you give, it is never enough. They would always try to guilt you into more.

I borrowed one of his lines. "If you don't like it, call the police."

Going to the airline counter, I am told my ticket is expired.

"Sorry. Good luck."

To make a long, frantic story short: Phone calls are made. Texts are sent.

"After a bit of commotion" -- as I described it in my journal -- I am put on the same itinerary as I had the previous day and I am told to hurry to the gate. I get there just as boarding commences.

I board and go to my aisle. I have never been so happy to get a center seat.

I finally allow myself the luxury of using the facilities and notice the abundant toilet paper and paper towels.

I feel like I am already halfway home.

--*-*-*-*-*

Okay. A short reintegration story to wrap up day 14. I am on the Bangkok-to-London leg of my trip home on Thai Airways and, unbelievably, I get an aisle seat. Wow. Life is pretty darn good.

As the plane gets ready to take off, I just can't believe it. I have hit the mega-jackpot of international travel. I have two empty seats next to me. I can actually lay down comfortably and sleep!

There is only one small issue to contend with. The fourth seat over is a sort-of, kind-of middle-aged lady who is plying that third seat with double pillows, double blankets, a thin newspaper and her pill bottles.

She is marking her turf.

I am willing to negotiate what to do with these extra seats, but I can tell by the furrowed creases in her brow it's going to be a hard sell.

Okay. Let's try a bit of the empathy approach.

"Ma'am, could I ask a big favor. I just escaped from the mountains of Nepal, and as you can see we have hit the jackpot of empty seats. I was wondering if I could lay down for a while and then -- "

I was about to continue that we could take turns resting, but she already had something to say.

"Look, I have had a long and tiring flight too and I specifically got this seat so I could have my personal space. Those two seats are yours and these two are mine!"

I told her something to the effect of "never mind," and patted her newspaper a little bit more roughly than I should have. "Enjoy your personal space."

I summoned all of my patience and self-control and whatever spirituality I had been able to muster from the East and West to stop myself from telling her what I thought of her, her personal space and what she could do with it. (Not wanting to get kicked off the plane was also a good motivating factor.)

I didn't ask to see where she purchased a second seat for her belongings. But I did share with her that the coat she hung on the back of the seat before us was three inches into my "personal space."

Welcome back to civilization!

I sleep reasonably well in my two-and-one-fifth seats and am served breakfast. When the stewardess comes around and offers a second cup of coffee I gratefully accept with an appreciative smile.

"Life is good!" I tell her.

She smiles in return, gives me a thumbs up and replies with a single word: "Happy!"

--*-*-*-*-*

Last journal entry of the trip:

"To be continued? Give me a while to forget the tougher moments and we'll see."

--*-*-*-*-*-*

Epilogues

Epilogue 1

How do I sum up my trip to Nepal? Of all of the competing emotions that constantly swirl in my head, how do I make sense of them and put them down on paper? At this moment, I don't think I can.

Of all the weeks, months and years of work that will fade into oblivion, I will never forget this adventure. Practically every single day, in some form or fashion, imagery of the Himalayas remains a part of my inner thoughts, my inner dialog.

I was a part of something that was bigger than myself. I fulfilled a lifelong dream to trek in the Himalayas. Would it be too cliché to say, I feel as though it is now a part of who I am?

I rarely broach the subject unsolicited, but I know it's there. It's something that adds a quiet sense of composure and self-confidence. You are impressed with my 20-mile bike ride? Why, thank you!

And there is that reassuring, unspoken conversation within: And you don't even know the half of it.

Epilogue 2

The mountains are many things to many people. There is the spiritual component of the adventure, the emotional aspects of the journey. I experienced the entire gamut of emotions on this trek and that is what helped make it so memorable and unique.

And then there is the physical component and my reflections back on the hardships encountered.

San Antonio has a moderate climate and I enjoy living here. Despite obvious exposure to the cold on this and previous outdoor adventures, there are many times when I have a hard time imagining the concept of "cold" when it is over 100 degrees outside.

But then winter comes to San Antonio for a few weeks each year. The old overcoat comes out of the closet, feeling snuggly warm against the frigid elements outside.

I take my shower for the evening and it's time to get out of the warm, luxurious water and I hesitate. I will be cold and wet. For a few moments, my creature comforts will be disrupted.

I have flashbacks to what the concept of cold is -- and I am not quite ready to head back to the reality of the Himalayas.

Epilogue 3

I take my evening walk through the neighborhood in near-freezing weather. I have my down jacket on as I walk through the lightly-falling mist. I imagine that I am in the mountains and beyond the mist lies the majestic peaks rising above me. I am back in Nepal.

The Himalayas live on in my spirit. The imagery is permanently imprinted on my soul.

--*-*-*-*-*-*

Epilogue 4

In 2015, a series of earthquakes hits Nepal. Chhiring sends me pictures of his family living under a tarp in Namche. It is the rainy season. It is not as romantic as it may sound at first.

I send out a message utilizing the mailing list I used during my trek to very delicately offer an opportunity to directly help out a Sherpa family in need, bypassing the aid agencies that were doing their best to deal with the devastation that had hit the region.

Chhiring, Yangee and Tenzing Doma in Namche Bazaar after the 2015 earthquake.

Generous support poured in. I was fortunate enough to be able to distribute thousands of dollars in direct aid to Chhiring, Kaji and their families.

Epilogue 5

I was pretty convinced I would never return to Nepal. This was a once-in-a-lifetime experience, something I will never forget and never regret doing.

But to go back and experience these hardships again? Taking everything into account, if I had to have placed a wager, I would have bet against it.

A year passed. And then another year. And with this time, the memory of the hardships started to fade, but the vibrant imagery of the mountains remained.

I start broaching the subject of returning to Nepal.

I receive absolutely no support from loved ones in this regard. They were all adamantly against it.

"You have already proved you can do it. Why do it again? No!"

After all, it would just be a do-over.

But I heard the siren song of the Himalayas and it called to me. Could I have one last hurrah among the tallest mountains on this planet?

The thought became intoxicating – again.

Slowly, I start regaining the support of loved ones. Once they saw my determination, I finally receive their blessing. They know how I am.

I contact Chhiring to see if he is willing to guide me back into the mountains. He is ready and willing.

The decision to return to Nepal also renewed my energies toward finishing up this transcript into a publishable format.

As I write these final words, I have just returned from my second trip to the Himalayas. When I got back home, I immediately hopped on the scales. I was shocked to see my weight had dropped 17 pounds. Yes, it was quite an adventure. But that is another tale yet to be told.

--*-*-*-*-*-*

Thank you for sharing this adventure with me. It makes the whole trip that much more meaningful to me.

Feel free to contact me regarding any questions you may have and I will do my best to answer. You can reach me at karlcsr@yahoo.com.

Please consider contacting Chhiring or Kaji if you plan to go to the Everest region. Their contact information is contained on the dedication page.

--*-*-*-*-*-*

Made in the USA
Middletown, DE
04 December 2018